DEDICATED TO THE MEMORY OF

RABBI ISRAEL GERSTEIN, Z"L
RABBI ISSAC MAYEFSKY, Z"L
RABBI DAVID TAMARKIN, Z"L
RABBI STANLEY WEBER, Z"L

DISTINGUISHED *MUSMACHIM* (RABBINIC ALUMNI)
OF THE HEBREW THEOLOGICAL COLLEGE
WHO WERE TAKEN FROM US DURING
THE PAST YEAR.
BY THEIR EXAMPLE WE LEARN THE IMPORTANCE
OF SERVICE TO COMMUNITY AND THE
MEANING OF *AHAVAT YISRAEL.*

"May their souls be bound up in the bond of eternal life."

THE COMING CATACLYSM

REUVEN P. BULKA
Second Revised, Edition

With a foreword by
Rabbi Dr. Walter S. Wurzburger

The Orthodox-Reform Rift and the Future of the Jewish People

 MOSAIC PRESS
OAKVILLE NEW YORK LONDON

Newly available from HTC Press: *OR SHMUEL Torah Journal*

5747-1986

The Hebrew Theological College Press
7135 North Carpenter Road
Skokie, Illinois 60077

Published by Mosaic Press, P.O. Box 1032, Oakville, Ontario, L6J 5E9, Canada. Offices and warehouse at 1252 Speers Roads, Unit 10, Oakville, Ontario L6L 5N9, Canada, and The Hebrew Theological College Press, 7135 North Carpenter Road, Skokie, Illinois, 60077 USA.

ISBN 0-88962-274-4 cloth
0-88962-275-2 paper

CONTENTS

Acknowledgments   Page 9
FOREWORD   Page 11
Introducton   Page 13
Section 1 – *The Background*
  Chapter 1
    The Reform Context   Page 19

  Chapter 2
    The Conservative Factor   Page 22

  Chapter 3
    Reform Today   Page 25

  Chapter 4
    The Positive Elements in Reform   Page 30

  Chapter 5
    Negative Aspects of Reform   Page 36

Section 2 – *The Crisis*
  Chapter 6
    The Coming Cataclysm – The Conversion Factor   Page 43

  Chapter 7
    The Coming Cataclysm – The Divorce Factor   Page 52

  Chapter 8
    Chaos – Can it be Avoided?   Page 58

Section 3 – *Suggestions*
  Chapter 9
    A Divorce Proposal   Page 65

  Chapter 10
    A Conversion Proposal   Page 73

  Chapter 11
    Can it Happen? Again?   Page 83

  Chapter 12
    Do Numbers Matter?   Page 93

Section 4 – *Projections*
  Chapter 13
    Future Reform   Page 101

  Chapter 14
    Future Orthodoxy   Page 108

  Chapter 15
    The Jewish Future   Page 118

  Bibliography   Page 125

Preface to the Second, Revised Edition

More than a year has passed since *The Coming Cataclysm* was first published. In that time, the major thesis of the book – that without intervention we are headed for a disastrous, permanent rupture of North American Jewry into two separate communities – has become a major focus of preoccupation among many who are deeply concerned with the future of the Jewish people.

The issues raised in the book were unfolding long before the book was written, and the concerns being expressed by Jewish leaders are not necessarily related to the publication of the book. The book happened to appear at a crucial and timely moment!

The cataclysm relates to the "integratability" of a large segment of the Jewish people. The problem of integratability relates to the Jewishness and legitimacy factors. Rabbi Irving Greenberg, the guiding force of CLAL (National Jewish Center for Learning and Leadership), has given a statistical face to the situation. Using conservative figures, he projects that by the year 2000 we will be confronted with 360,000 problematic conversions and at least 200,000 whose patrillineal connection will lead them to assume they are Jewish, but who are not Jewish according to Halakhah. Additionally, by the year 2000 there may well be 200,000 who are burdened with the difficulties of questionable legitimacy, and thus marriageability. All these are very low estimates, as far as I can see.

The figures add up to the non-inegratability of at least three-quarters of a million of the Jewish population belonging to the Reform and to its left. The issue is more than numbers. With the Reform population comprising so many theological problems, the traditional community will slowly, but ever-so-surely, distance itself, then separate, and may ultimately divorce from Reform in its entirety. They will do this to avoid all problems related to identity and status.

According to Lawrence Schiffman, in his worthwhile book, *Who Was a Jew?*, the final break between mainstream Judaism and the Christian sect came when that sect's population became predominantly non-Jewish. All other differences were tolerated, but the Jewishness factor could not be ignored. That same scenario is rapidly developing in modern Reform. This evolving reality prompted the sounding of the alarm about *The Coming Cataclysm*.

The book has elicited many interesting and varied reactions. Some question my use of the word "coming." They insist the cataclysm is already upon us. Others question whether anything can really be done to ward off the tragedy. They doubt whether the leaders of the community will be able to transcend petty politics and vested interests. And, thankfully, there are a significant number who insist that something can and must be done.

Obviously, I align myself with those who are actively working to resolve the situation and I do so, even more strongly, precisely because of the skepticism and apathy of others.

The road to resolution is long and arduous. Any final resolution must be preceded by authentic dialogue. But even that first step is evolving at a painfully slow pace. That first step is so important if we are to check the sociological drifting away of one group from the other.

We must be hopeful, and insistent, that the potential tragedy never comes to pass. This is a crisis of our own doing and it is therefore our collective problem to solve. What is needed is the proper combination of confidence and anxiety; confidence in our destiny, anxiety about that very destiny. Hopefully, the energy created by our anxiety will ultimately justify our confidence.

Reuven P. Bulka

ACKNOWLEDGMENTS

There are a number of people who have had a helping hand in the development of this work. Professor Conrad Winn extended the original invitation to address the topic of this book at a gathering in Temple Israel. That experience drove home the urgency of the issues herein discussed even further and served as catalyst for my setting the thoughts down on paper.

The Rabbi at Temple Israel, Sanford Marcus, was generous in making available to me much Reform literature relevant to this volume. Dr. Richard Wagner offered some useful comments which have tightened up parts of the book.

My secretary, Blanche Osterer, did her usual efficient job in typing the manuscript, and Jean Naemark was helpful in many aspects of preparing the work.

I am honored by the foreword of Rabbi Dr. Walter S. Wurzburger, a distinguished leader of the Jewish Community and outstanding thinker, who himself has been in the forefront of confronting the issues central to this volume.

Sharon Katz Mayne has greatly enhanced this work with her artistic front cover. Not only the final product, but also her enthusiasm for the challenge of making an attractive front cover, are greatly appreciated.

Finally, I express my thanks to Howard Aster of Mosaic Press for his interest in the work, and his assuring the highest standards in all aspects of its publication.

To all those who have helped make this volume possible go my heartfelt thanks. I hope that whatever affect the book has will justify their efforts.

FOREWORD

by Rabbi Dr. Walter S. Wurzburger

The growing polarization of the Jewish community constitutes a clear and present danger to the unity of the Jewish people.

Well-intentioned pleas to embark on all-out efforts to assure our survival as one people will hardly be of any avail. What divides us are not only ideological differences but irreconcilable conflicts about the nature of Jewish identity and status. We are faced with a situation where frequently Jews who abide by the Halakhah will have to disqualify as marriage partners many individuals who would be perfectly acceptable to Reform Judaism.

There are no easy solutions to these agonizing problems. The difficulties arise not from institutional concerns, parochialism, or lack of good will, but reflect fundamental theological differences.

Rabbi Reuven Bulka, one of the most dynamic leaders of the North American rabbinate, deserves the gratitude of all segments of the Jewish community for articulating the issues so cogently and compelling us to confront them squarely. What is so refreshing about his approach is the emphasis upon the need for developing the kind of options which could be adopted by the various religious movements without compromising the integrity of their respective positions.

Religion is neither politics nor business. In the spiritual sphere one cannot settle issues by making concessions. Total commitment is the very essence of a religious attitude. But what is needed is the ability to transcend institutional or denominational concerns in the quest for solutions that will enchance the welfare of the entire Jewish people.

History shows that in various areas of endeavor, important breakthroughs were achieved once the proper questions were asked. Whatever reservations we may entertain about some of the specific recommendations of the author, he has placed us in his debt for his brilliant formulation of the questions which must be put on the agenda if we are serious about creative Jewish survival.

It is my fervent hope that *The Coming Cataclysm* will create a climate of exploration and soul-searching from which there will develop the insights required to avert the fragmentation of the Jewish people.

INTRODUCTION

The concern of this volume is the future of the North American Jewish community. Any neophyte observer of the Jewish scene who has watched how Judaism has unfolded over the last few years in North America has no doubt been able to pick up the predominant theme of North American Jewish life, namely increasing polarization. This polarization is not merely along the traditional lines of Orthodox in one direction and Reform in another direction. Polarization can be seen within Orthodoxy, within Conservative Judaism and within Reform.

Polarization is an extreme form of expression of differences. It is a case of ideological differences becoming isolationist, if not antagonistic positions. Thus, it is not unlikely that within the next decade or two, the relationship between modern Orthodoxy and the predominant Orthodoxy of the day will be somewhat akin to the relationship presently prevailing between Conservative Judaism and Orthodoxy, a relationship characterized in the main by overt antagonism, mud-slinging, and invective-laden diatribe. Traditionally centrist Orthodoxy is moving further and further to the right, and modern Orthodoxy is being left behind, and becoming, by its very isolation, more closely allied to right-wing Conservative Judaism.

This development poses challenges of its own, but is not the particular focus of the present volume. The center of attention in this volume is the growing polarization between Orthodoxy and Reform. To be sure, Orthodoxy and Reform were always diametrically opposed to one another. Nothing about the original ideological gap has changed. If anything, the gap has widened by dint of the continued reintrenchment of the respective positions of the Orthodox and Reform camps, not to mention the movement to the right within Orthodoxy which is proceeding at a far quicker pace than the rightish trends within Reform and which carries with it a parochialism and disdain for any groups to the left.

What is of concern is that, if present trends remain unchecked, the policies which prevail within Reform Judaism and the commensurate reactions which they will surely evoke within the Orthodox camp, and most probably within the mainstream Conservative movement, can very likely result in a cataclysmic split within the North American Jewish community. It is unlikely that this cataclysmic split will occur tomorrow, but it is not unlikely that it will unfold within the next generation or two. This split may result in the total renunciation of a significant number within the Jewish community by another group, and the separation-cum-divorce of these two movements into a mainstream Judaism, and a new religion, the name of which is at present a matter of guesswork.

What follows in this presentation is an historical overview of the background of the problem, an examination of the problem itself, a projection of the repercussions of the problem, and some suggested strategies to avoid the cataclysm. The reader may not be convinced that the situation is as serious as suggested herein, but it is my firm belief that if action is not taken quickly, effectively, and decisively, we are heading towards a disaster of massive proportions which the North American Jewish community simply cannot afford.

This is not an abstract treatise; it is intended not to be. It is not written from the ivory tower, where theological jargon is employed. Instead, this is written from the vantage point of the trenches, from the vantage point of grass roots reality.

It is based on perceptions of reality that go beyond what takes place in the academic study halls, talmudic academies, or Rabbinical conventions. It is based on the observation of what is unfolding on the Jewish main street in North America.

What allows me to be presumptuous enough to assume license to even talk about this very sensitive, potentially explosive topic? Briefly, I graduated from an Orthodox Rabbinic Seminary, serve as an Orthodox Rabbi in an Orthodox congregation in the capital city of Canada, and have been privileged to maintain this position for over fifteen years. In these fifteen years, I have met Jews of all stripes, who attach to themselves every possible label that Judaism offers in its smorgasbord of theological choice. I see before my eyes the very polarization that is the topic of this work. I have also seen, and continue to see first hand, the dangers of further polarization, and entrenchment of this widening gap, that is the result of the vastly different policies of Orthodox and Reform Judaism. I have visited other communities, talked to Rabbinical colleagues, spoken to responsible community leaders in many cities, and have become almost obsessed with the dangers which lurk and which must be met head-on.

And, just a short while ago, at the invitation of Professor Conrad Winn, I addressed the members of Temple Israel in Ottawa on this topic. That opportunity forced me to crystallize my thoughts, and the overwhelming response to the presentation, both in terms of numbers present and reaction to my remarks, further reinforced my own feeling of urgency concerning this problem.

No doubt, there are other Rabbis who are as aware, and who have an equally sensitive finger on the Jewish pulse. This is not intended to be the final word on the issue, just the first word, and perhaps not even the first word, since undoubtedly there have been many others who have voiced the concerns contained herein. However, it is my contention that every Jew in the forefront of communal leadership must place this issue on the "front-burner" of priorities. We have the tendency to wait for the crisis and then to react, but in this instance, as in most other instances of crisis, once the crisis is before us it is usually too late to act effectively.

Still, even considering the crisis situation, I approach this work with trepidation. The matters to be discussed are delicate; perhaps, in the view of some, private, in-house matters that should not be debated in public. There are two reasons why I proceed in spite of the hesitancies. One is that very little about any aspect of Jewish life is a strictly non-public matter. The information that appears in the popular media is often inaccurate and misleading, so setting the record straight is useful, if not necessary. Second, there has been much subterfuge, dishonesty, ignorance, and failure to inform an unsuspecting public which has contributed greatly to the developing chaos. Effective action can arise only if there is a strong demand for corrective measures to put the floundering ship of Jewish destiny back on course.

There are those who may quarrel with my impressions of Orthodox, Conservative, and Reform Judaism, what they stand for, what they have achieved, and the danger of the volcanic mix, the interaction or lack of it between these trends within Judaism. My presentation is not intended to exclude all other presentations, and also not to preclude the rush of defensive, apologetic, or even legitimate counter insights into the realities of these three trends, or, as Neusner calls it, sectors. However, I do believe that what is contained herein is a legitimate presentation of the mainstream reality of today, and based on that, the potential dangers for tomorrow. In the debate which will hopefully ensue, I only hope that all commentary will not be diatribe, but rather a serious confrontation of the issue in a constructive manner, and geared towards a resolution of this escalating problem.

What is the problem? What is the nature of the problem? In what inheres the movement towards a solution? These are the questions which will be confronted in the ensuing pages.

Reuven P. Bulka

SECTION 1
THE BACKGROUND

CHAPTER 1
THE REFORM CONTEXT

Like other trends within Judaism, and perhaps even more so, it is difficult to speak of Reform Judaism as if it is monolithic. Rather, there are different brands of Reform, spanning a vast gamut from the left, which borders on being totally out of the pale, all the way to the right, which has a close kinship with left-wing Conservative Judaism.

The Reform movement as we know it today is linked directly to its humble beginnings in the 19th century, in the climate of emancipation. The basic thesis of Reform, and that which separates it radically from Orthodox Judaism, is that the Bible is not the eternally valid word of God. Instead, the Bible reflects the primitive ideas of its own age, and is thus not binding on later generations, and possibly not even relevant. This rejection of the Bible as the eternally valid word of God may seem to be just a simple theological concept, but its implications are wide ranging. It means that the Talmud, which Orthodox Judaism views as *the* definitive explication of the Bible, or the written law of God translated into everyday application via the oral transmission–the oral tradition which is the Talmud, is little more than an historical buffer. It is one way of interpreting the Bible, but certainly not the definitive way. As a matter of fact, in the Reform conception, since the Bible is not God's inalterable word, but rather the initial attempts to form and formulate an Israelite community via a specific code, any attempts toward building upon this initial exercise must almost by definition be improvements upon the original theme. We have here at work the theological counterpart of the theory of evolution, in that the Jewish religion is continuing to evolve from its humble, pristine beginnings, and each generation furthers the evolutionary process. But the evolution into the 20th century is an improvement over the 19th century and etcetera backwards.

Orthodoxy, on the other hand, sees the Revelation at Mt. Sinai as the event of events, the wellspring of pure unadulterated Torah, unaffected by human foibles such as forgetfulness, subjectivity, laziness, capitulation to convenience, or moral laxity. Biblical interpretation seeks to get back to the roots, recognizing that each generation is one step further removed from Sinai and the roots of tradition. For Orthodoxy, Mt. Sinai is the eternal focal point; for Reform it is no more than a point of departure, and that, with a very diluted view of revelation itself.

In the conception of Reform, therefore, Judaism is in a constant state of refining itself, improving itself, adapting itself, and should never be stultified into a particular code of observance that becomes obligatory for the millennia. Within this theological construct, many of the norms of the culture in which Reform operates become defining characteristics of the Reform Judaism of the day. Thus, originally, Western aesthetic and decorum standards, a much abbreviated, and church like – if you will – service, delivering of the sermon in English – something which originally was an intense issue dividing the Reform and the Orthodox, but which has become a more or less accepted practice within all trends of Judaism today; choir singing with organ accompaniment, and the emphasis on the language of the country being the language of the service rather than the original Hebrew text, were all part and parcel of the initial Reform amendments to what had up until then been standard Jewish practice.

The Judaism of the day, in the Reform view, was to be judged by the values of the prevailing culture. It is thus no accident that many of the elements which characterize the church service, such as the aforementioned shortened prayer service, when compared with the longer traditional service, and choral singing with organ accompaniment, amongst others, became basic norms by which Reform was identified.

Along with the liturgical changes, a more basic conception of the Jewish way of life was also introduced by Reform. This followed the same general pattern, that of obliterating those elements within Judaism which gave it a distinctiveness, or in the pejorative sense, a separateness from the world at large. Thus, even at prayer services there would be no kipa (head covering) worn, nor would the traditional prayer shawl (talit) be part of the actual dress for prayer. This was considered anathema. We have not yet even reached discussion about tefilin, the distinctive phylacteries, which probably, to a certain extent, were a non-issue, since the traditional times for wearing the phylacteries, the weekdays, were not times when one would be likely to find a Reform service in operation.

The adherence to dietary laws was another distinctive feature of Jewish life which the original reformers scoffed at, and considered totally non-essential to the lifestyle of the Jew.

Perhaps the most radical departure, looked at from the perspective of the 20th century, was Reform's total renunciation of any yearning for a return to Zion. This was manifested firstly and foremostly by a declaration that such belief was an unconscionable betrayal of the host country which opened its doors to the Jews, and secondarily reinforced via the deletion of all reference to return to Zion in the prayer liturgy. The fact that Reform congregations are invariably referred to as temple, stems from the Reform view that yearning for the restoration of the Temple is theologically absurd and politically disrespectful. There would be no new Temple in Jerusalem; instead the messianic fulfillment is reached through the building of small temples in every area where Jews are found. The Reform congregations, in this view, were the new temples. Thus, even though today Reform has made a drastic about-face relative to the basic ideology which gave birth to the name "temple" as part of all its' synagogue names, nevertheless the preface Temple, as in Temple Sinai, Temple Israel, or Temple Beth-El, etc. etc., is still a basic identification component of any Reform synagogue.

It is not my intention to enter into a lengthy analysis of the motivations of the early reformists, whether they indeed saw their efforts as saving Judaism, or as being the Jewish conduit to universal respectability via the divesting of all Jewish uniqueness. Such analysis is at the present time, and for the present purposes, basically irrelevant, since whatever face one places on these motivations, there can be no doubt that the normative Judaism of the day from which Reform broke, what is commonly referred to as Orthodox Judaism, stood then and stands now as uncomprisingly opposed to the Reform world view, its implications and repercussions.

One can take the cynical view that the original reformers had made up their mind that the time had come to strip Judaism of its particularistic and parochialistic labels and practices, and it was time for the Jew to become part of the greater society rather than live in the ghetto or shtetl. Only then would Jews be free of the anti-semitism menace. What followed after that was a theological justification for all this, in the form of rejecting the notion that the Bible was immutable, God's word which could not be contradicted or modified. Conceivably, if Reform were to recognize that this was the original basis for the Reform of today, and would also recognize that the anti-semitism factor has not been neutralized by Reform, it would perhaps indulge in more serious soul-searching.

But for the Orthodox, it really does not make much difference; except for the possibility that putting a cynical face on anything and everything that Reform has done from its inception cannot help but make the abyss that separates Orthodox from Reform Judaism today an unbridgeable gap. And that, in the final analysis, opens the door for tragedy.

CHAPTER 2
THE CONSERVATIVE FACTOR

The original founders of Reform Judaism, were they alive today, would probably not recognize the movement that they had given birth to, at least in certain circles. However, before presenting some of the defining characteristics of modern Reform, it is interesting, as a footnote to history, to observe that the Conservative movement in North America was originally conceived as a buffer to bridge the gap between the Reform movement and its continual tilt towards the left, and the Orthodox with its bent towards the right. The Conservative movement initially was a theological D.M.Z. dedicated to bringing Reform closer to Orthodoxy! Solomon Schechter, a magnum force in establishing the Conservative movement, came from England to the United States and started what is now referred to as the United Synagogue. The United Synagogue in North America is identified with the Conservative movement. However, in England, the United Synagogue is the umbrella organization for all Orthodox congregations. Verily, when Schechter came to the United States, he used the same name he had been acclimatized to in England, the United Synagogue, to launch his movement. It was a movement toward Orthodoxy, as his choice of name indicated. History, however, has played a trick on Schechter and his intentions. The United Synagogue in America is today totally different in philosophy and direction from the "primordial" United Synagogue in England. Additionally, the Conservative movement is today not so much a buffer as it is a movement of its own, which theologically is in between the Orthodox right and the Reform left.

However, the Conservative movement, by virtue of its original intent as being a bridge, has up until this moment not evolved a definitive theological system. On the contrary, the Conservative movement is essentially still a movement in flux, with many Conservative Rabbis bordering on modern Orthodoxy, and others bordering on Reform. Conservative Judaism can boast of some great Talmudic scholars, and some significant contributions to Jewish thought. However, in its theological conceptions, it shows the ambivalence that comes from having sympathies for Orthodoxy whilst at the same time understanding and trying to reform Reform.

Thus, for example, Conservative Judaism speaks of the importance of keeping kosher as a sacred value, but at the same time can countenance individuals maintaining the practice of kosher at home, but abdicating on such practice outside the home. This somehow or other combines an in-house Orthodoxy with an out-of-house Reform. This type of compromise may be palatable to many who find keeping kosher at home manageable whilst maintaining the rigidities of kashruth at business lunches and parties fraught with too much difficulty. But such a position is theologically almost self contradictory. Either the practice of kosher is a value, in which case it is valid in all instances and obligatory in all situations, or else it is nothing more than a nice option, if that, in which case it is not mandatory even in the home.

However, the theological and historical aberrations notwithstanding, Conservative Judaism can probably, from the hindsight of historical perspective, claim some credit for at least keeping Reform within the Judaic matrix until the 1980's. Though it certainly did not succeed in narrowing the gap between Reform and Orthodox Judaism, Conservative Judaism did at least succeed in checking the Reform drift away from Judaic identification. Of course, the argument can be made that whatever check in the drift which did occur was due to factors within Reform itself, but the likelihood is that without the expressed concern of a significant portion within the Jewish community, the rethinking that went on within Reform would certainly not have unfolded the way it did.

Today, in another ironic twist, Conservative Judaism, whilst philosophically more oriented towards Orthodox Judaism, finds itself politically in the same boat as Reform Judaism. Specifically as pertains to the situation in Israel, where the Rabbinical infrastructure is Orthodox, both the Conservative and Reform movements have long yearned for recognition and equal opportunity in matters of a religious nature. However, this status having been denied to them, they have more or less aligned themselves in a common cause to infiltrate the so-called Orthodox Rabbinic establishment. It is too early to tell whether and how this political alignment will eventually affect Conservative theological thinking, although the guess is that the primary thinkers within the Conservative movement, leaning as they are towards traditional Jewish expression, will not allow politics to derail Conservative Judaism from its conceived thrust.

In the final analysis, it is unlikely that the religious establishment in Israel will bend towards legitimization of even the Conservative movement in totality, and the alignment of Conservative with Reform makes this likelihood, however remote, well nigh impossible. So, the alliance, and whatever benefits may accrue in terms of a common stance, probably will land up harming the Conservative Rabbinate in Israel, and will certainly not enhance the standing of the Conservative Rabbinate amongst the Orthodox in North America.

So much for the Conservative movement and its role in the past as well as its role in the present. It cannot be dismissed as a legitimate possibility, but the present realities do not indicate that the Conservative movement in the 1980's will be able to play a role in bringing together, in whatever shape or form, the

Orthodox and Reform movements, or at least preventing a total estrangement. Conservative Judaism remains an attractive option simply because it is a skillful blend of traditionalism and Americanism, and will for the foreseeable future command a large following.

But it is doubtful whether this following is vocal enough and zealous enough to stem or create tides. Of the three major movements, it would seem as if the Conservative movement has the least passion, although this is admittedly a subjective judgment which is difficult to justify scientifically. The very nature of Conservative Judaism, as a blend, involves the idea of theological as well as psychic compromise and adjustment, with a neutralization of fervor via the capitulation to social realities in the expression of norms outside the home. There is, to be precise, a right wing trend within Conservative Judaism which contradicts this very analysis, but as yet this element has not become the mainstream of Conservative Judaism, though this is certainly not an impossibility in future years. For better or for worse, the main protagonists in the arena of Jewish destiny in North America at the present time are the Orthodox and the Reform. What is Reform Judaism today, and how does it differ from the Reform of yesterday?

CHAPTER 3
REFORM TODAY

Reform Judaism today is in many ways quite different from the Reform of yesteryear, or, more precisely, the original Reform. Whereas Reform had its roots in the rejection of Judaic norms, today one may find many Reform individuals and groups who are actually wrestling with tradition, and fulfilling precepts, albeit in the Reform manner, which were totally rejected just a short while ago. Thus, one can find Reform individuals today who would don a prayer shawl and wear the tefilin, something which was unthinkable to the original fathers of Reform, who distanced themselves radically from the magical amulet which they saw as unscientific, non-logical, and totally irrelevant. Today, in many Reform congregations, it is not forbidden to wear a kipa (head covering). Instead it is optional, and some people have taken it upon themselves to exercise that option.

Nevertheless, it should still be stated that people who naturally gravitate towards Orthodox or Conservative congregations, and who for whatever reason happen to attend a Reform service, invariably state that they find the service to be somewhat akin to a church service, and lacking all religious fervor that they would normally expect at a prayer service.

Insofar as the prayer service itself is concerned, there is a movement afoot, the extent of which is still too early to guage, of a return to some of the original texts. Many Reform individuals pride themselves in the reintroduction of Hebrew language prayers into the liturgy. To someone who has prayed in Hebrew for decades, this may seem to be a very insignificant adjustment, but viewed from the vantage point of history, it indicates a tendency within certain Reform circles to return towards tradition.

This return is already hinted at in the dramatic shift of direction which is embodied in the Columbus platform of 1937, in contradistinction to the Pittsburgh platform of 1885. The Pittsburgh platform renounced the archaic vestages of Judaism and instead placed a primacy on Judaic ethical norms as being the manifestation of Jewish expression. It also at the same time gave up all aspirations for what was then referred to as a Palestinian homeland. The Columbus platform, by contrast, came full circle, and recognized the role that tradition plays within Judaism, and if it did not embrace tradition, at least it did not totally reject it out of hand as the Pittsburgh platform originally did.

It would be misleading to state that all Reform congregations today adhere to the spirit of the Columbus platform. There are a number of trends within Reform, the one trend leading further left, and bordering on an ethical humanism which is stripped of all ritualistic norms and in some instances even of belief of God; the other moving closer towards traditionalism, and even occasionally arguing that Reform could use a code of observance.

The ethical humanism trend is evident in such findings as that more than one-quarter of Reform Rabbis do not believe in God in "the traditional Judaic sense," that 44% of Reform seminarians identify themselves as agnostic, that only 4% of Reform seminarians believe in God in "the more or less traditional Judaic sense," and that less than one-fifth of Reform congregants believe in God "in the more or less traditional Judaic sense." When such belief is chucked out of one's lifestyle, ritual practices which are nourished by this belief in God are suffocated at the source, and one is left with an ethical humanism tenuously linked to the prophets of yesterday but more strongly rooted in the humanistic ethics of modern vintage. This trend is perilously close to dissociating from Judiasm en toto.

On the other side, the rightist trend in Reform has made its presence felt with significant forcefulness. That, within the Reform context, one should even speak about a code of observance is heresy.

Reform was originally based on the notion of continuing evolution of religion and religious practice, and the total rejection of the stultifying codification of religious rules onto paper. The thought of putting down a code of Jewish practice, Reform style, somewhat like a very much abridged code of Jewish law, would make of that type of Reform an Orthodoxy! This would be a coming full circle from the original rejection of the Orthodox ethos and its being set down in print as a code of law.

Whereas the original differentness of Reform was most salient in its attitude towards Israel, Reform today has done an about face. Instead of being negative or even neutral about Israel, Reform today is in the forefront, even the vanguard of concern for the State of Israel. For any responsible Reform leader today to suggest a reversion to the Pittsburgh platform negativity concerning the State of Israel would be almost out of the question. However, it should be stated that Reform allegiance to Israel today takes the shape not of a religious commitment to a State of Israel sanctified through a promise by God to Abraham and fulfilled in generations past. Rather, it takes the form of a commitment to the survival of the Jewish people and the feeling that survival is best effected through a Jewish homeland in Israel.

It is therefore not surprising that in the affirmative stance towards Israel which is evinced by Reform, there is a detachment from the argumentations which would place legitimacy on the claim to Israel via a Biblical promise. Reform in general distances itself from references to the West Bank as Judea and Samaria, and does not identify very strongly with the right of Israel to the West Bank and Gaza.

This is nothing more than logical within the Reform framework, since it evokes a similar neutrality-cum-negativity concerning the basic Judaic practices which are suggested in the Bible, such as the stringencies concerning the observance of Shabbat and festivals, the dietary regulations, and other normative practices. It would thus be inconsistant for Reform to reject those norms, and yet affirm the historical nexus between the land of Israel and the Jewish people via Biblical promise. If the Bible is not to be taken as eternally valid and immutable, this must pertain across the board, including in matters relating to Israel.

With all this, Reform too has its Neturei Karta, a fringe group which distances itself from Israel and rejects any involvement with the destiny of the State of Israel. The people of this group would want to wish Israel away and just concentrate on living within the free democratic atmosphere of North America.

On the ritual side, there are significant numbers within Reform that observe such practices as lighting candles for Shabbat. This would include many people who have come to Reform from Orthodox and Conservative backgrounds and have found the Reform congregations more attractive to them for whatever reason. Also it may be true of those assimilated Jews who have come back from nowhere to become involved in Jewish observance. The adherence to candle lighting, however, is not the same as the candle lighting that would go on in an Orthoprax Jewish family. Here it is done as an identification ritual, in order to feel Jewish. It is certainly not done as a divine imperative actualized as a fulfillment of God's will or of a Rabbinical edict. As a matter of fact, if those who lit the candles were aware or thought that they were doing so to fulfill a Rabbinic ordinance, or that they were reciting the sanctification prayer known as the kiddush to fulfill the Rabbinic explication of a Biblical imperative, it is quite likely that they would drop the practice like a hot potato and look to other ways for identity affirmation.

This, however, should not be dismissed as a religiously irrelevant expression. The very yearning for return, the attempts of many within Reform to plant roots within Judaism, is a healthy desire. Whilst the theological underpinnings of this expression may pose problems for Orthodox theology, the alternative to such identity search, being totally oblivious to identity questions or searching for identity within other ethnic or religious contexts, is a less desirable alternative.

The religious leader who heads the Reform congregation today probably purchases meat from a non-kosher source. That person may even purchase this meat on a Shabbat, compounding the breach. However, the Reform congregation per se may still have some measure of kashruth observance operative within the synagogue confines. This does not mean that the Reform congregation adheres to the letter of the kosher law, but it does make some concession to the notion of keeping kosher. Thus, one may find a congregation within Reform ranks which observes what is known as "Biblical kashruth." This means that whilst the chicken or meat that is served is not kosher, nevertheless the congregation insists on refraining from those items which are biblically proscribed, such as pork, horsemeat, and the like.

If one surveys the adjustments that have been made within Reform over the course of the 20th century, one finds an interesting pattern at work. Reform from the very outset was greatly influenced by the surrounding culture. The norms with which it invested the Temple service were a reflection of the accepted value systems and aesthetic ideals of the church. In the 20th century, and particularly in the past few decades, there has been a noticeable shift in American thinking, away from the melting pot ideal, and towards the expression of ethnicity. In previous decades, the accent was on being American. Pressures were placed on individuals and groups not to dress differently, not to behave differently, but to be American. Reform was probably in the vanguard, ideologically, of this principle. Therefore, its theological expression reflected the notion of sameness as an ideal. The service, which even in the early stages of emancipation approximated to a great degree the prevailing church service, continues to do so. Additionally, Reform dress codes and behavior codes were nothing more or less than American.

But much has changed over the course of the past decade and a half or two. Perhaps as a result of the civil rights revolution, in which, ironically but at the same time understandably, Reform lent moral and tangible support, Americans have shifted away from the melting pot ideal towards the idea of ethnic expression. The Negroes of America rejected the idea of any form of discrimination because of color, and this carried with it the equivalent rejection of discrimination based on creed or religion. Instead, each race or creed was to be allowed its freedom of expression unimpeded, and uncompromised by the pressures to kowtow to the amorphous American ideal.

The new American ideal was for each group to maintain its uniqueness. This drastic switch in direction literally took the carpet out from under Reform. America now actually glorified that which was different. Sameness became mundane, differentness became exotic. When National Geographic reported on a segment of the Jewish community, it was the most noticeable and obvious Jewish community that it pictured, the Hasidic. When Ironsides decided to have an episode relevant to the Jewish community, it showed a very religious community which became terribly depressed when its Torah Scroll was stolen. The media, which to a certain extent has always been a barometer of what is fitting and proper in society, was a most embarrassing rejection of the Reform notion of conformity.

This in large measure explains why there has been such a drastic change in the Reform outlook on religious expression. If the networks, the magazines, and other popular media organs see nothing wrong with showing phylacteries and fringes of the tallit, as well as ear locks, then there is nothing wrong with having them, or wearing them, or aligning with the ideals which actually espouse these precepts. For Reform to turn around and actually adopt these outer forms as part of their lifestyle would be too drastic a change, almost a leap from Reform into Orthodoxy or Conservatism. But not to tolerate these forms would be to make Reform less understanding of its Jewish brethren than the American public. Such a reality could not be tolerated. Thus, the new Reform accommodation, which has an open mind and theoretical, though in most instances probably grudging acceptance, of these norms as part of the Jewish mosaic, even though they do not think it actually pertinent to their own selves and their own lifestyles.

On balance, then, there are essentially two trends within Reform today, the one inching towards Orthodoxy at a turtle like pace, rejecting Orthodox philosophy whilst at the same time swallowing some of the best that Orthodoxy has to offer, and on the other hand a trend towards further disengagement from Judaic tradition, and the espousal of the universalistic norms clearly identified with ethical humanism.

CHAPTER 4
THE POSITIVE ELEMENTS IN REFORM

Orthodoxy today is becoming, in general, more parochialized, concerned about matters of internal import relating to its own situation and to the situation in Israel, as well as the plight of Jews the world over, most notably the Jews in the Soviet Union. In such centers as New York City, which more than any other locale attracts greater Jewish salience, there is an abundance of Jewish candidates for all levels of positions, and an exceedingly high rate of Jewish involvement in the political process.

Those who vie for positions of power are desperate to have their picture taken with a prominent long-bearded Rabbi, in order that they should be seen as identifying with Orthodox causes and therefore eliciting a favorable ballot response from the Orthodox community. New York City is probably the exception in terms of Orthodox Jewish activism, though this is not to imply that there is no Orthodox Jewish activism outside New York City; only that it certainly cannot compare in intensity with the New York City Orthodox political activity.

Without attempting to make a value judgment or to sound pejorative, the impression is that Orthodox activism in general relates to Orthodox concerns.

An Orthodox tabloid might recommend voting for a specific candidate because of a particular stance towards the gay community or to capital punishment.

A positive feeling towards Israel would be a prerequisite for any candidate in need of the New York City vote. Even those who may have a prominent track record concerning Israel, suddenly, for political expediency if nothing else, become very skillful at espousing Jewish causes, often outjewing the Jew, posturing a militancy which particularly the Orthodox love to hear. Support, on whatever level of government, for religious institutions, can also go a long way for any political candidate.

In the main, all these are issues which impact on the Jewish community in particular. This should not be taken as a negative judgment concerning Jewish communal priorities. The nature of the political process is inherently parochial, catering to individual needs. In an area of high unemployment, a candidate who promises, realistically I might add, the prospect of jobs, is likely to win. In an area highly concentrated with women voters, someone with a positive stance towards women's issues is likely to do well. In an area where an anti-nuclear energy posture is likely to have a devastating impact on the community, a candidate who is in favor of nuclear limitation may have difficulty whilst the candidate who skirts around the issue or is vehement in insisting on the need for nuclear energy will probably do better. In an area densely populated with Negroes, a candidate who is strong on civil rights and champions the cause of minorities is likely to do better than a bigot. On the other hand, in areas of white supremacist bigotry, a bigot will do better.

There are various shades and nuances in the political process, but the essence of political gamesmanship is trying to convince your clientele that you can best serve their interests. The Jewish community, where it is strong as a community and can muster a large number of votes, has banded together to exercise its political muscle. It has learned the lesson of the American way very well, and should certainly not be condemned for taking full advantage of the opportunities that have been placed before it.

The Reform movement, in its political activism, does not blatantly project in a parochial manner. It is invariably on the liberal side of issues, be they social action, civil rights, the attitude towards women and gays, etc., but its posture is more a reflection of what it thinks should be the American reality, rather than a self-serving position. As a matter of fact it usually works in reverse. What is perceived to be a liberal trend within the American political mosaic may be adopted as a Reform stance, rather than vice versa. Orthodox politics projects Orthodox priorities onto the political arena, whereas Reform politics translates the liberal trends of America into liberal theology. Of course, this is a generalization which has exceptions, but the perception that the generality holds more often than not nevertheless still pertains.

One cannot help but admire Reform activism with regard to issues of social import. Reform is in the forefront of issues involving separation of church and state, issues of civil liberties and human rights, issues involving the administration of justice, and has been involved more than any other Judaic trend in the issue of nuclear disarmament. It may very well be that nuclear disarmament is the major looming issue in the next decade, and the Orthodox, leaning as they are towards a rightist posture not only theologically but also politically, are unlikely to publicly stampede for a stance which, in its perception, will weaken America vis-a-vis its Russian adversary. The Reform attitude towards this is ostensibly more militant in terms of disarmament and less than militant with regard to the America versus Russia intrigue. Still, Reform's official position on nuclear disarmament is fair-minded and well balanced. Whether one agrees with their positions or not, one has to admire the fact that Reform has been involved in the issues and has tried to project an intense concern for the future of America, indeed of all humanity.

A second issue in which Reform has distinguished itself over the last number of generations has been in its support for Israel. This is not to say that Orthodox or Conservative Judaism has to take a back seat to Reform, but that Reform has made definitive, and in the context of its past history, quantum strides, in its support for Israel. Still, it is particularly painful to sometimes hear Reform threats to withdraw its financial support for Israel if Israel is not forthcoming in recognizing the Reform Rabbinate as a legitimate representative of the Jewish people. One would hope that Reform support for Israel is unconditional, and one gets the impression that this indeed is so; that when push comes to shove, support will more or less remain at the same level.

However, the residue of Reform's original opposition to the reestablishment of a Jewish State still haunts the Reform community. Even though two-thirds of Reform youths say that giving to the United Jewish Appeal is the most important ingredient in firming their Jewish identities, fully half of Reform youth claim that Zionism is never a topic of discussion in their homes. As a result, only two out of every three Reform youngsters are solidly pro-Israel, with many of the remaining one-third harboring strong anti-Israel feelings.

Tangible and moral support for Israel has also been compromised on occasion by a greater tendency within the Reform movement to criticize the Israeli government, particularly the government of former Prime Minister Menachem Begin, in matters which it finds disagreeable. In the issue of whether American Jews should publicly disagree with and criticize the government of Israel, one tends to find the Orthodox leaning towards silence, and the Reform leaning towards vocal expression. The Orthodox view is undoubtedly rooted in the fear that anything said publicly against Israel may be manipulated by some politicians with adverse affect. These politicians, molders and reflections of opinion, need not fear any charge of bias against Israel, since they can readily point to prominent Jews who share their views. This has in effect happened more than once.

On the other hand, the Reform view is that by not speaking out against what Israel is doing, the public is given the impression that Jews do not care when moral issues are involved concerning the actions of their own people, whereas with regard to other peoples they would be quick to react and to criticize. The Reform view is that by showing sensitivity to the moral issues, standing four square in the forefront of moral rectitude, whilst at the same time supporting Israel ideologically, they do immense good for the perception of the Jew within mainstream American society as a loyal, concerned citizen.

The Israeli incursion into Lebanon to rid it of terrorists is probably as good a litmus test as any of this differential between the Orthodox and the Reform. My impression is that the bulk of criticism leveled against Israel publicly, within the Jewish community, came from people generally identified with the Reform element. Even here, however much one may disagree with the notion of public criticism of an already politically beleaguered Israel, one should take note of the dynamics involved, dynamics of sensitivity, concern, and a tradition of commitment to ethical and moral excellence that is the heritage of Israel. Thus, even in what may be perceived by some to be disagreeable expression, the roots of this expression are in a long standing tradition to which Reform, however unconsciously or subconsciously, has shown its commitment.

Finally, there is one more area of Reform expression which deserves mention, if not elaboration. This is that the Reform movement, more so than the other movements within Judaism, is more inclined to talk about God. Reform is interested in the conception of God and the meaning of religion, and is concerned about the religious factor in everyday life. Perhaps because Reform is on an identity search, searching not only for itself but also for its linkage with the Judaism of past generations, and its place in the Judaic fold, it is going back to the fundamental principles of Jewish belief. And there is nothing more fundamental than understanding the meaning of one's relationship to God. What in Orthodoxy may be taken for granted, and what in Conservative Judaism may not be so relevant, being that the social context is of more concern, in Reform the issue of belief is very much a lively topic.

Here again, the cynic might say that whereas Orthodox practice orients around talking to God, Reform distances itself, and focuses on talking about God. Nevertheless, such cynicism should not blind us to the fact that the Reform concern about God really focuses on the source of our being and values, and as such it is deserving of more than a flippant dismissal. All too often those to Reform's right, in sanctimonious self-justification, only entrench themselves further in what they are doing, and fail to give credence to the validity of what others are doing; even saying implicitly, if not explicitly, that since their basic philosophy is wrong, everything that the Reform do is also wrong, and nothing they do is worth observing or learning from.

It should be noted that though there is much discussion about God in Reform, the thrust of most of that discussion leaves much to be desired. More than one-quarter of the Reform Rabbinate do not espouse the traditional belief in God, a miniscule amount of Reform seminarians believe in God in the traditional sense, with almost half being agnostic, and more than 80% of Reform congregants do not believe in God in the traditional sense. Translated, this may mean, in crude terms, that they do not believe in the Orthodox God, but believe in the Reform alternative, or in no alternative. This being the case, the talk about God in Reform may not be such a good thing after all. It may indicate the need to start from scratch, and start afresh, to establish the theological parameters of Reform Judaism divorced in theory, if not in fact, from its original tradition.

Still it should not be ignored that there have been direct benefits to Orthodoxy from the sensitivity to religious categories evidenced in Reform. Much has been written about the "born again" phenomenon within Judaism, commonly referred to as the

Baal Tshuva movement, the infusion of large numbers of returnees from assimiliation to full identification with Judaism, and often to the expression of Jewish norms to the extreme. Many institutions of learning have been set up just for these types of individuals, and significant articles, if not whole issues of journals, have been devoted to the Baal Tshuva phenomenon.

It is interesting to note that of the returnees, members of the Baal Tshuva movement, more come from the Reform movement than do from the Conservative. On the one hand, one would have expected that the Conservative movement, with its closer adherence to tradition, should be more of a repository of Baal Tshuva potential. However, in the final analysis, Reform's predilection for religion, and its concentration on theological matters, has awakened a religious quest within its constituency, often to the point of going further right than had been envisaged.

Thus, Orthodoxy should at the very least grudgingly grant to Reform the status of being an effective holding pattern, which often awakens a religious impulse in heretofore dormant souls, who find their way, slowly but surely, and sometimes suddenly and completely, to the very right within the Jewish matrix. Precisely because there is a significant flow between Reform and Orthodox Judaism, and a visible influx from Reform ranks into the Orthodox fold, and vice versa, is it even more imperative to explore the relationship between Orthodoxy and Reform and the portent for the future.

The point has been made by some insightful observers that Reform has performed a noble service for Orthodoxy. Were there no alternative, the many who find Orthodoxy unpalatable would have had only an "either-or" choice, either an unbearable form of Judaism or no Judaism at all. Too many would have opted for the latter alternative, thus creating a significant-cum-massive drift away from Judaism. The Reform alternative has forestalled much of this drift by offering Judaism with less ritual, Judaism without ritual, Judaism without God, even Judaism without Judaism, among other options. The Conservatives, too, figure in this equation, but to a lesser degree than the Reform since tradition is still a potent factor with the Conservatives and one has the impression that fewer Conservatives would have opted out of Orthodoxy with no other alternative. One may even argue that whilst the Reform option prevented a greater drift, the Conservative option, with its modernistic traditionalism, has actually spawned a flow away from Orthodoxy!

By way of mathematics, it is generally estimated that 40% of the nearly six million Jews in North America are "peripherals," outside the mainstream or sidestream of Jewish life. The remaining 3,600,000 are about evenly divided among the Orthodox, the Conservative, and the Reform. (*Time*, in its October 8, 1984 issue, p. 76, reported there were 1,100,000 Reform, 1,700,000 Conservative, and 416,000 Orthodox. That is

34

surely not an equal division, but the Reform numbers are consistent with the present thesis.) Reform is the frontier on the left, the holding pattern before the great abyss. Its constituency, in broad terms, is the 1,200,000 identifiable Reform and the 2,400,000 unidentified. Most of the unidentified, if they do come back gradually, would make Reform their first stop. Optimistically, Reform can impact on 60% of the North American Jewish community, so that Reform's role in the size and shape of tomorrow's North American Jewish community must not be underestimated.

Many a Hasidic shaliach, of the missionary type, have indicated that they feel more at home with Reform Jews, who always evoke a religious sensitivity, as opposed even to Conservative and Orthodox Jews, who they often find antagonistic to the ideas they attempt to project. They make the classic distinction between Reform Jews and Reform Judaism. They insist, quite correctly, that there is no such thing as a Reform Jew. Either one is a Jew or one is not a Jew. There is, however, a reality called Reform Judaism, which Hasidism, as much as any other element within Orthodoxy, rejects as a viable option. However, they do not throw out the baby with the bath water, and keep open the lines of communication with those who espouse the philosophy of Reform but who, by virtue of that espousal, do not become condemned or ostracized. Reform can be a conduit to increased commitment.

CHAPTER 5
NEGATIVE ASPECTS OF REFORM

From an Orthodox point of view, the most negative aspect of Reform is Reform itself. That is to say, the very fact of Reform, with its rejection of the Torah as the eternally valid word of God, is objectionable in extremis. Naturally, all that emanates from this objectionable Reform premise is equally objectionable. However, even if one were to hypothetically suspend theological judgment concerning Reform, there are certain elements within the Reform dynamic which remain objectionable.

The Reform infatuation with the liberal side in social issues of current import almost guarantees that Reform will remain nothing more than a mirror reflection of social values, even if these values stand in contradiction to hallowed norms. Additionally, even if these norms may be contrary to what Reform will have thought independently, the likelihood is that Reform will capitulate to the social pressures to espouse the stance that is identified as liberal.

The two examples that are immediately striking are the women's liberation issue and the gay liberation issue. In the women's liberation issue, Reform has been in the forefront of equalization, even to the point of having women Rabbis heading some of their congregations. Actually, from an Orthodox point of view, one could make the argument that this is not even a great problem. A Reform Rabbi does not do what an Orthodox Rabbi does, namely adjucating matters of legal import, and serving as a teacher of Jewish law. Instead, a Reform Rabbi performs pastoral duties, delivers sermons, leads in prayers, etc.

However, considering the fact that the Reform prayer service is not the standard liturgy, and that it really takes the form of selected readings, having a woman Rabbi leading a Reform congregation is probably no more objectionable from an Orthodox point of view than is a woman singing in a mixed choir in a Temple setting.

In the strict Orthodox view of things, a Reform prayer service is nothing more than a social gathering to recite together. Bits and pieces are siphoned off from the traditional prayer service, but the standard ingredients which comprise a traditional prayer service are missing. The Reform service is seen as a reading exercise of minor significance. No one should lead, so it matters little who really does.

In the rush to equality, the Reform have, to a certain extent, overstepped their own belief system. One looks almost in vain for mention of tefilin in Reform texts. At most, there is a grudging acceptance of phylacteries as an identification symbol, but, especially amongst those who still endorse the original Pittsburgh platform, the tefilin are certainly not part of the Reform lifestyle. They are magical amulets with no spiritual significance. Yet Reform sees nothing wrong with women putting on these phylacteries (tefilin), and staunchly defends this right. Thus, at the same time and in the same breath, Reform takes a somewhat neutral cum positive stance towards the institution of phylacteries in general. Why project woman's right to an observance which has already long been frowned upon in the Reform movement? It is, in effect, a lip service gesture which really turns out to be meaningless— endorsing the woman's right to observe that which is considered extraneous to Reform Judaism proper.

It is also debatable whether Reform permissiveness regarding abortion is a humanistic position, or whether the sensitivity to the women's rights issue in abortion has been achieved at the painful and cruel expense of the sanctity of all human life. In an ironic twist, Reform sensitivity to the moral and ethical quality, Reform espousal of the liberal, humane position has given birth to a distorted set of values concerning the unborn child. In effect, the path of Reform has led to the rejection of Reform!

Then there is the matter of the attitude towards homosexuality, and towards the so-called gay liberation. Precisely because Reform rejects the eternal bindingness of the Bible, it has no trouble with the fact that the Bible considers homosexuality a matter of capital import. It can therefore endorse, and even sponsor, a gay congregation. However, the question here is whether being in the vanguard of "freedom of choice" in this issue does not undermine the basic substructure of values which is important even in the Reform movement. The necessity of family, the importance of proliferation, the maintaining of a tradition of values and transmitting it to the next generation, is verily a part of Reform. However, by espousing such values as gay rights, or by allowing for such values to become officially sanctioned within Reform, Reform is in effect saying that the value of individual choice countermands the value of futuristic responsibility. Even if Reform may not say this either explicitly or implicitly, it would not be too difficult to understand why the public would receive such a signal. It is one thing to understand the gay situation; it is another to endorse it, or to give it sanction.

Whilst original Reform evinced some form of theological consistency, in that there was an across-the-board rejection of the Bible as God's word, and an insistence on ethical humanism, Reform today has to wrestle with a new reality, an ever expanding definition of what is correct, proper and conscionable. What would have been considered a great breach in the era of emancipation, e.g., homosexuality, is now considered perfectly acceptable. Does this, at once, continue to project an ever increasing liberalism within Reform, whilst at the same time destroying the Reform base for continuity? The rush to espouse what is a public norm may be self destructive for Reform.

It therefore may be crucial for Reform to take a much more sober and detached attitude to societal norms, to contemplate what could never have been fathomed originally, namely to radically reject a societal norm that has been accepted by the general public; this, for reasons of self preservation if for nothing else. However, by doing so, Reform will have in a sense Orthodoxized itself, by saying that there are limits beyond which it cannot go.

Birth rate is also a major problem within Reform. If one considers that the Modern Orthodox family has, on the average, 3 children, and the very Orthodox 5 or 6 children, and that the North American Jewish Community's overall rate of multiplication is only 1.67, well below zero population growth, then those to the left of the Orthodox must be at sub-zero multiplication in too many instances. How else can this overall low figure, next to the relatively high figure for the Orthodox, be explained? To have a general birth rate of two, for every family of six children there would be two families with none; or for every family of 5, there would be three families with only one child. This, coupled with the usually more advanced age for marriage and child bearing amongst those to the left of the Orthodox, means that not only are Reform generating less children, but they are also losing generations. Projected over several decades, for instance, those who marry and have children in their 20's, who in turn marry and have children in their twenties, will have forged three generations at the same time as those who have children in their thirties forge only two generations. Over the long range, the fertility factor does not augur well for Reform. If Reform does maintain its percentage of affiliates, it will be mainly through the numbers they are able to attract from the "peripherals," and those to the right who are disenchanted with the Conservatives or the Orthodox.

Consistent with Reform's all-encompassing identification with society-at-large is the fact that Reform has the highest rate of assimilation amongst the major trends within Judaism. This means assimilation in the statistical and non-statistical senses. In the statistical sense, it relates to an ever increasing rate of intermarriage between Jews and non-Jews. More than one out of three Reform congregants in the early 20's is married to a spouse who was born non-Jewish, and, in this age group, one out of four is married to a spouse who has not converted.

In the non-statistical sense, it is the increase in the number of Jews who do not care at all about their Jewishness. Two-thirds of Reform congregants admit that they remain Jewish simply because it is the most convenient thing to do. If such individuals do marry others who are Jews, it is purely by accident and not by specific design. These couples would still, even though both are Jewish, reject the notion of religious education, would observe holidays such as Christmas and Easter as the American way and reject the parochialism of Passover and Yom Kippur, and generally give no tangible expression to their Jewishness, such that their children may likely never know that they are Jewish, and will be divorced from involvement with the Jewish community. These are the unwritten statistics which are more dangerous and much more threatening for the future of the North American Jewish community than the measurable intermarriage statistics.

Many within Reform claim that they are different from the *Orthodox* as opposed to the *Orthoprax* in name only, but in actual practice both eat the same unkosher food and desecrate the Shabbat equally. This is reminiscent of the old joke that the difference between the Orthodox and the Reform is one block – the Reform park their cars on the Shabbat right in front of the Temple, the Orthodox park one block away. The Reform claim consistency to their behavior. There is nothing wrong with driving on the Shabbat, they say, and they have nothing to hide. The Orthodox, who know it is wrong but do it anyway, are hypocrites, the argument goes.

The Orthodox would no doubt counter that there is no greater hypocrisy than negating a norm or destroying a precept in order to avoid the guilt of having sinned. It is better to keep the law on the books, even if it is only honored in the breach, so that those who want to follow halakhic guidelines know what is proper, and those who do not follow at least remain aware of what is missing in their lifestyle. When the time comes, and those who do not follow desire to return, the past guilt can become the impetus for present fulfillment.

Reform presently is an odd mix of many varieties. In Israel, Reform keeps kosher for its functions, so as not to disadvantage those who observe Jewish dietary law. In North America, kosher is not "in." There is no practical or theological consistency in this or other areas of traditional ritual practice. Anyone can, and many do create their own rules and procedures. With no uniform approach, it will be extremely difficult for Reform to evolve its own traditions. The tradition of every person for his or her own self is not a perpetuating model.

To a certain extent, an argument can be made for the proposition that Reform Judaism is a different religion, sharing with the other trends within Judaism a similar last name, namely "Judaism," but having a different first name, i.e., Reform. According to this view, the different first name really is more indicative of the reality than the common second name. Reform emulates more a church model than a synagogue model, is continually distancing itself from a mainstream Judaism that is becoming more militant, whether it be within Conservative or Orthodox ranks, and often espouses a lifestyle of non-observance which is on the brink of religionlessness. True, there are movements back to tradition within Reform, but these movements are Reform in name only. Bluntly, they are a new Orthodoxy.

The flirtation with self-destruction that characterizes many elements within Reform is certainly not what many have conceived Reform to be, namely an extension of Judaic tradition that continually adapts to the generations. If the ultimate adaptation is the total divestment of the Judaic cloak, then Reform in too many instances is successful. But it would be misleading to itself to label this as a brand of Judaism. Undoubtedly the thinkers of Reform, assuming their sincere intentions even if they may be branded as misguided, would not have wanted Judaism to end with them or with their grandchildren. However, in many instances this is precisely the case. There are vibrant areas within Reform, but numbers wise, Reform is this side of a disaster area.

Reform is thus caught on the horns of a great theological dilemma. On the one hand, the movement towards the right, and the legitimization of tradition, carries with it the ultimate dangers of becoming a new Orthodoxy, yet a type of Orthodoxy none-the-less. On the other hand, there is a drift within Reform towards total departure from Jewish ranks. If this is to unfold, then it will have stamped Reform Judaism as a signal failure in its attempt to revitalize Judaism and guarantee its posterity. Orthodox theologians may argue that the best contribution Reform can make to history is to acknowledge that the Reform experiment was futile, doomed to failure. Jews should recognize this lesson of history and never deviate to the extent which Reform recommended, but should rather adhere to tradition as the benchmark for Jewish survival and growth.

Whatever the case, and however entrenched Reform may be in the American psyche, the problems raised herein are ones which should plague Reform consciousness, and should elicit a respond-to-crisis reaction which is both personally and communally responsible.

SECTION 2
THE CRISIS

CHAPTER 6
THE COMING CATACLYSM –
The Conversion Factor

If in fact Reform is heading in two divergent paths, the one towards Orthodox style though not essential Orthodox traditionalism, and the other towards assimilation into the American Mosaic, then there is probably little that one can do to save those who are on the brink of the plunge into secularism, nor is there anything that one would want to do for those who are on the way towards renewed traditionalism save to encourage and accelerate that process. However, this scenario of diversions is too simplistic, as well as probably not a matter of the immediate moment, but something which will unfold gradually, and probably not in our time. In the meantime, however, sneaking up from behind and lurking in the background, is a dangerous potentiality which can create a cataclysmic split between Orthodox and Reform Judaism, and result in a divorce of ominous proportions threatening the future of Judaism and the Jewish people in North America, if not the entire world.

This is not the first instance of theological differences amongst segments of the Jewish population. We have had our Sadducees and Pharisees, we have had our Karaites, we have had our Sabbateans, and we have had our Frankists. However, this is probably the first time that Judaism has been so polarized that today it is not enough to identify oneself by saying one is Jewish. One needs to place a defining adjective in front of that label, and to clearly state whether one is Orthodox, Conservative, Reform or other, of which there are endless possibilities. Even the fact of such entrenched division is not justification enough for being alarmist about the future of the North American Jewish Community.

If unity because of diversity is not possible, unity in spite of diversity should ideally still be achievable.

However, there are distinctive policies which are being pursued by Reform, and which are at the same time utterly rejected by Orthodoxy, as well as by significant elements within Conservative Judaism, which do not bode well. The first issue of concern can be broadly subsumed under the title "Who is a Jew?" This controversial question, which had its heyday in a confrontation in Israel a number of years ago, has had its share of copy in the official organs of Orthodox, Conservative and Reform Judaism, but had not really been a headline grabber in recent times aside from its mention in coalition politics. More recently, the "Who is a Jew" issue has occupied center-stage in Israel, with significant spill-over, and often bitter reverberations, in Jewish communities across the globe.

Within the Reform Rabbinate, there is a lingering debate concerning the question of whether Reform Rabbis should be given license to officiate at mixed marriages. By mixed marriage is meant the marriage of a Jewish person with a non-Jewish partner, *without* any form of conversion, even Reform. There are those within Reform who would argue that the idea of Rabbis being allowed to officiate at marriages between Jew and non-Jew has a logic of its own. That logic is that if we allow Rabbis to perform only marriages between Jewish partners, be they Jewish by birth or by conversion, it then places implicit if not explicit pressure upon the non-Jewish partner to convert should the Jewish partner insist on having a Rabbi officiate at the wedding; and for some strange reason, many do so insist. However, by so doing, we will have contravened the basic Judaic opposition to forced conversions. Rather than countenance, or encourage forced conversion, which is also a breach of that hallowed principle of "freedom of choice," it is better to allow Rabbis to officiate at a marriage between a Jew and non-Jew, so that free religious expression can be maintained and the basic Jewish objection to religious coercion of any sort is not compromised.

Presently, about 40% of Reform Rabbis will officiate at mixed marriages with no conversion of the non-Jewish spouse, and more than half of the remaining 60% of the Reform Rabbinate who themselves do not officiate will refer mixed marraige couples to Rabbis who do. Thus 70% of the Reform Rabbinate gives tacit or explicit approval to mixed marriages. However, to this point in time, whilst there is strong support within the Reform Rabbinate for officially allowing mixed marriage, such permission has not been forthcoming, and Reform Rabbis have not been given carte blanche to officiate in any marriage.

In spite of this, as has been pointed out, there are many Reform Rabbis who will unhesitatingly officiate at mixed marriages. They will do this autonomously, and on occasion they will do it together with a priest or minister, and have no qualms about it. Reading the society section of the New York Times is ample enough evidence to convince any doubting Thomas (or Cohen) that this is more than just a passing occurrence that happens rarely. It is all too prevalent, and a disturbing feature of Jewish society in North America.

Let us assume, for argument sake, that the mainstream Reform position, if one may be so bold as to propose such a reality, is that ideally a marriage officiated at by a Reform Rabbi should at the very least be preceded by a Reform administered conversion of the non-Jewish spouse. What does a Reform conversion entail and what is its' status among the Orthodox?

Essentially, a Reform conversion is a reflection of Reform ideology. Since Reform ideology is more interested in history, ethics and morals, and very liberal with regard to ritualistic norms, it stands to reason that education towards conversion within

44

Reform will take on the trappings of lessons in Jewish history, Jewish culture, and Jewish practice as something to be aware of, with some loose pledge of allegiance to the Jewish corpus. Absent from such conversion will be the insistence upon adherence to Judaic ritual practice. It would be ridiculous for Reform to insist that converts be holier than they, that converts be obliged to observe the dietary laws, refrain from material ceativity on the Shabbat, don the phylacteries on a daily basis, recite the prayers regularly, fast the entire Day of Atonement, etc., etc. If the Rabbi who is supervising the conversion most likely does not observe these practices, how can these even be suggested for the prospective convert?

Thus, what in Orthodox Judaism is an essential component of conversion, namely "Kabalat haMitzvot," or the commitment to observe the commandments, is non essential, even non existent in Reform conversions. A Reform convert may learn about phylacteries and dietary laws, but such learning is merely looking through a telescope backwards into archaic practices which are no more in vogue.

Then too, with rare exception, two major ingredients within conversion, the circumcision for males, and the ritual immersion in a *mikvah* – a body of water gathered in place through very exacting procedures outlined in Jewish law, will invariably be missing from the Reform conversion process.

Reform has also been ambivalent at best with regard to circumcision. Although circumcision was recommended, still Reform would allow a circumcision performed by a non-Jewish doctor, a procedure which from an Orthodox view renders the circumcision suspect, if not invalid.

The feeling that circumcision was barbaric was somehow neutralized by the reality that circumcision was for a long time common medical practice even for non-Jews. It would be difficult to sustain the argument that circumcision is barbaric if even those who are not obliged for religious reasons to be circumcised nevertheless voluntarily have circumcision for medical reasons. Today, there is an ongoing debate in medical circles about the need for circumcision. There are those who say it is unnecessary, whilst there are those who insist that it is useful and should continue to be a regular routine. There is little doubt that an argument can be made for circumcision being beneficial on hygienic grounds, the question merely being whether it should be mandatory and whether there are ways of maintaining the health benefits that accrue from circumcision without circumcision itself.

Reform is more interested in the substance of the issue, whether one is circumcised or not, than with the full covenantal implications of circumcision. Whilst halakhah clearly states that only those who are part of the covenant can perform the covenantal act of circumcision, Reform is satisfied if the child is circumcised, no matter by who, and there is some religious ceremonial attendant to the surgery. In the case of a non-Jew seeking to convert, Reform has certainly *not* been insistent on the need for circumcision, taking the view that it is not necessary. And, with prospective converts who have already been circumcised medically, but there remains the requirement of a conventai blood-letting of a trivial amount of blood, almost all Reform Rabbis would dismiss this as barbaric and totally unnecessary. After all, the would be convert is circumcised.

For many to the right of Reform, the thought of marrying anyone not properly circumcised even if born Jewish, is unfathomable. The more Reform allows for circumcision by non-Jews, the more problems are created for those who insist on marrying only those who, by religious definition, have been appropriately "covenanted."

The notion of ritual immersion has also long been frowned upon within Reform circles. Reform has rejected the ritualistic legislation concerning the menstruant woman, and mikvah is a non-existent institution, or has been up until recently within Reform. There have been instances where Reform Rabbis, conscious of Jewish tradition, have tried to impress this tradition upon the prospective convert by taking that convert to a mikvah. It is certainly harmless when compared with a circumcision, and is a potentially meaningful spiritual experience. However, from an Orthodox point of view, such a gesture, much as it may be lauded as a move towards traditionalism, is nevertheless still legally problematic.

To set the situation into proper relief, one must be aware of the basic requirements for conversion within Orthodox tradition. Aside from the very tricky area of *kabalat hamitzvot*, the acceptance of the responsibility to observe the commandments, there is the need for a convenantal act, be it circumcision or *hatafat dam brit* (the letting of the blood of the covenant), and ritual immersion, both of which must be witnessed and attested to by qualified witnesses, namely individuals who adhere to Jewish tradition, i.e., they observe the Shabbat and other Judaic norms.

It is understandable that only those who adhere to tradition are qualified to testify that the traditional requirements have been satisfied, as is the rule that only those who do not have a history of lying are reliable witnesses. This by definition just about excludes all Reform Rabbis, who do not qualify as adhering to Jewish tradition because of their rejection of all the hallowed practices which have been enumerated previously. Thus, a Reform Rabbi who courageously encourages a prospective convert to try the mikvah, makes an emotionally significant gesture, but which theologically borders on the irrelevant from an Orthodox point of view.

Orthodox Judaism, which uncompromisingly rejects Reform Judaism, must by definition equally and commensurately reject

Reform conversion. This is not merely a politically expedient judgment. It is an unavoidable judgment which is made about any conversion procedure which does not conform to the Code of Jewish Law, and no matter who performs it. The fact that all Reform conversions do not meet the legal requirements makes this an across-the-board judgment. It should be noted in this regard that most Conservative conversions would be subject to the same view. What is left after all this is the inescapable conclusion that by Orthodox standards, a Reform conversion is an exercise in futility, and the person who assumes the state of being Jewish subsequent to such conversion is, by Orthodox standards, as non-Jewish as before. In Jewish law, the state of an individual's Jewishness is directly dependent on the Jewishness of one's mother. Thus, if the mother is Jewish at the time of birth of her child, the child is Jewish. If not, the child is not Jewish, unless there is a *legitimate* conversion either through the adoptive procedure, where the Rabbinical court assumes responsibility and entrusts the child to the care of the Jewish parents, or the child, at a later stage, when reaching responsibleness, decides to join Jewish ranks.

Although it is small comfort, this legal construct allows that where a non-Jewish male marries a Jewish female, the issue of such union will be Jewish since the mother is Jewish. These types of conversion, when a Jewish female marries a non-Jewish male, are usually less prevalent than the reverse, when a Jewish male marries a non-Jewish female.

Non-Jewish males are generally lesss likely to convert, due to the circumcision factor, a painful experience which adults would rather avoid. Of course, within Reform this is not a key issue since circumcision is not mandatory for conversion. A second reason is that because the children of such issue are Jewish anyway, since the mother is Jewish, there is less pressure for conversion, a pressure usually quite forceful among Jewish families desperate to have Jewish grandchildren. In a union between a Jewish male and a non-Jewish female supervised by a Reform Rabbi, and with the conversion of the Reform stripe, the children of such issue, by Orthodox definition, are non-Jewish. Even though the parents may raise the child in a Jewish environment, may consider themselves Jewish and identify totally with Jewish causes and with Jewish destiny, the fact remains that from an Orthodox point of view, the child of a Reform converted non-Jewish mother is still a non-Jew.

When you consider this mix, namely the greater incidence of Jewish males marrying non-Jewish females, the higher rate of marriages between Jew and non-Jew prevailing amongst Reform, the fact that a Reform administered conversion is, from an Orthodox point of view, considered invalid, the sum total adds up to utter confusion. If the situation continues, and expands as per the indications, it will be very difficult to tell who, within Reform congregations, is Jewish, and who is not. When the reality hits home that the mix in a Reform congregation is so great that the Jewishness of member families is not guaranteed, and with time even remote, there will be more reluctance to have any form of sharing between the congregations. Especially for families within Orthodoxy, who are particularly sensitive to intermarriage and the compromise of Judaic values, this only increases exponentially the likelihood that there will be an increasingly impregnable barrier between the movements, and a separation of Reform from Judaism itself.

We are living today in a fluid society, where we meet people of all persuasions in our regular daily activities. This more than anything else probably is the most significant factor in the high rate of inter-marriage. In previous generations Jews hardly met non-Jews. Their movements were restricted to the confines of the ghetto or shtetl, such that intermarriage was a very remote possibility. In the present free flowing situation, Jews meet non-Jews all the time. They meet on university campuses, they meet on the job, they meet at cultural and sport activities, they meet literally everywhere. It is precisely this type of social mix that has exposed a greater number within the Jewish community to the non-Jewish population.

In a relatively recent survey of American Jews, close to half felt there was nothing wrong with intermarriage, and among the younger generation (20-29 year olds), more than two-thirds felt that way. My guess is that the overwhelming majority holding to this view are from the 60% of Jews who are either Reform or to the left of Reform. Down the road, then, we are looking at a likely increase in the number of intermarrieds in Reform from the present one in three. The problem of "Who is a Jew?" within Reform will thus probably get much worse before it gets better.

If the social structure invites cross cultural interchange, it stands to reason that this very interchange process will also apply to Orthodox Jews meeting Reform Jews (much as I hate these terms), and vice versa. The shock that obtains when one legitimately thinks one has found a nice mate, who is also Jewish thank God, only to be told by the Rabbi who will officiate at the wedding that according to Orthodox law the mate is not Jewish, is too overwhelming to describe in words. Needless to say, it opens up a tremendous range of difficult circumstances, soul searching, and even ultimate disintegration of the potential marital union. What immediately goes through the mind of the Jewish spouse is having to deal with a complicated situation, including a mother-in-law who is non-Jewish according to the Rabbi's definition. But the main problem is the supposedly Jewish but in fact non-Jewish mate, who has always lived under the impression of being Jewish, and is now in a terrible state of shock, disbelief, and understandable anger. That such a person should refuse to be reconverted is understandable. Thus, even though an Orthodox Rabbi may have the option of reconversion, it is often more difficult to convert someone who thinks he or she is Jewish, rather than someone who knows he or she is not Jewish and needs to be converted.

Based on the stark reality of all the problems that are posed by the mess that exists in the conversion situation, it would not be surprising if before too long it became common practice for Orthodox families to recommend to their children not only that they not get involved with non-Jews, but also that they *not get involved with the Reform community*.

Not wanting their children to intermarry, they will insist that their children avoid any "high-risk" social environment. This is unfolding to some degree right now, but with time it can easily become entrenched policy. "Don't go to the Temple, it is full of goyim!" To prevent the possibility of eventual marriage, the Orthodox would swear off any connection with Reform from childhood. One need not be a brilliant sociologist to see what this can lead to. In simple terms, it can lead to a cataclysmic division within Judaic ranks, the splitting off of Orthodoxy from Reform to the point where they evolve not only as two separate life styles, but as two separate religions, and never shall the twain meet.

Reform has doubtless been affected by the exposure to Orthodox categories. Ample evidence for this is the significant trend in one Reform group towards more traditionalism. Should the Orthodox turn their collective backs on their Reform counterparts, Reform will likely do the same, and go further away from any connection with tradition, and with those who have rejected them. The separation would become a permanent divorce. Of course, there are those within Orthodox ranks who would probably say "so be it," but the "who cares!" attitude is an irresponsible one, and certainly does not project the communal concerns that Jews have always possessed, and, I feel, that intrinsically they still possess.

Some Reform leaders have recognized the great attrition that is taking place within the Reform fold, and have taken to serious study of the situation, to come up with recommendations that will address the situation. One of the suggestions has been to go back and re-examine the matter of patrilineal Judaism. As mentioned before, Judaism is essentially matrilineal, in that the child of a Jewish mother is Jewish and the child of a non-Jewish mother is non-Jewish, if there is no valid conversion. At the same time, the father's contribution to the child's status is not non-existent. Whether the child is a priest (Kohen), Levite, or Israelite is dependent on the status of the father. A Priest who marries an Israelite woman would have children who themselves are Priests. A Levite who marries an Israelite woman would have children who are likewise Levites. An Israelite male who marries the daughter of a Priest would have children who are Israelites. Thus there is an interesting mix, in that whether one is Jewish or not depends on the matrilineal connection, whereas the status of

49

one's Jewishness, i.e., whether one is Priest, Levite, or Israelite, is dependent upon the patrilineal connection.

In this context, much debate has been sparked by the suggestion thrown out as a trial balloon by the Reform, that the child of a marriage between a Jewish male partner and a non-Jewish female partner be considered as Jewish. This would, for all intents and purposes, destroy the concept of matrilineal Judaism, which has been a hallowed tradition throughout the generations.

Attendant to the suggestion that Judaism become also patrilineal is the parallel insistence that this can only work if the child of the marriage between a Jewish male and a non-Jewish female is raised as a Jew. However, one can see the chaos that easily results from this haphazard guideline. If the child is raised Jewishly enough for whoever it is to decide, then that child will be considered Jewish, and if not, not. This places subjectivity and arbitrariness into a situation which demands precision and exacting standards, rather than loose and imprecise ones.

The patrilinealism issue has taken a recent radical turn, with the passage of a patrilinealism resolution by the Central Conference of American Rabbis. The resolution, in part, asserts that "The child of one Jewish parent is under the presumption of Jewish descent. This presumption of the Jewish status of the offspring of any mixed marriage is to be established through appropriate and timely acts of identification with the Jewish faith and people." Dissident groups within Reform, notably the Reform Rabbis Council of Toronto, have put some qualification on the CCAR resolution. The Toronto Reform group has stated that "If the father is Jewish, the child is psychologically and sociologically distinct from the child of two non-Jewish parents. The child has a claim on his/her Jewish heritage and should be raised as a Jew, if so desired. Participation in appropriate ceremonies such as conversion, brit milah, female covenant ceremony, bar/bat mitzvah, determined through consultation with the Rabbi can lead to an exclusive identity."

The "participation in appropriate ceremonies such as conversion" clause would seem to reject the patrilineal resolution. After all, how appropriate is conversion if the child, by Reform definition, is already Jewish?

The Toronto statement manifests a divergence of views in Reform ranks, but that divergence is minor compared with the repercussions of a patrilineal policy on the North American Jewish community.

The problems previously enumerated, and emanating from different answers to the question, "Who is a Jew?" projected by Orthodoxy and Reform, are immediately compounded. Fears of gradual separation of the Orthodox from the Reform, are now replaced by the more sober and realistic prospect of an instantaneous, radical separation of Orthodox from Reform.

The wisdom of the patrilineal Judaism suggestion deserves more than passing comment. The obvious benefit from patrilineal Judaism is that the perceived attrition within Jewish ranks would be checked, or at least that is the thought. Instead of a situation where a Jewish male marries a non-Jewish female and is lost to the fold, as are the children, with the concomitant diminishing affect on the numbers within Judaism, we would instead welcome these children into the ranks of the Jewish community, and thus not merely stem the numerical losses, but actually swell Judaic ranks.

However, given the accepted tradition that the child of a non-Jewish mother is non-Jewish, hiding behind the smoke-screen of a new definition of who is Jewish and thus having greater numbers of Jews is nothing less than voodoo magic. Whether it is through sprinkling holy water, or pronouncing a new doctrine, and thus presto, abra cadabra making of a non-Jew a Jew, the facts remain the same, the reality is the same, and only our perceptions have become distorted. If burying our heads in the sand, or saying of something black that it is white, are effective means for changing reality, then this is an excellent solution. But as long as the dilemma is not confronted at the root, and the solutions offered do not get to the guts of the issue, all that will be achieved is superficial window dressing which gives the illusion of solution but really is an exacerbation of the problem, even the cause of Jewish communal disintegration.

CHAPTER 7
THE COMING CATACLYSM
The Divorce Factor

The matter of conversion is only one of two volatile issues that threaten the Judaic fabric in North America. The other is perhaps even more volatile because the problems that are created are sometimes insoluble. It is the problem of divorce, and the Reform practice relative to divorce. According to Jewish law, and this has applied since Biblical times, when a husband and wife decide that the time has come for the parting of ways, for whatever reason, the marriage must then be dissolved via a ritually precise instrument called a *get*, or a bill of divorce.

Jewish law from time immemorial, based on Talmudic precedent, was quite understanding with regard to grounds for divorce. One was not forced to concoct a phony adultery in order to legitimize a split. Even if one found a more desirous mate, this was considered grounds for divorce. What this means is not that the Talmud recommends that individuals continually search out the terrain for someone who is more attractive or more inviting, but that where an individual reaches the stage that another potential mate is more desirable, then it is obvious that the original mate has become less than desirable, and it is not fair that the couple should be forced to maintain the union. This type of open-endedness concerning divorce is potentially dangerous, and much advantage can be taken from it.

However unbalanced, it is much better to have a marriage institution which is not locked in prison-like, but rather where one continually renews the covenant, and does not take tomorrow for granted because yesterday was okay. Guaranteed life tenure has its drawbacks in the work force, and also in marriage. Until relatively recently, Jewish families suffered little from divorce related problems, so that the relatively loose requirements for granting a divorce have not impacted negatively on Jewish family life.

Assuming, then, that marriage has reached a terminal state, and the couple desire a split, so that they can each go their own way, Jewish law necessitates a get. Most individuals are aware, or at least assume, that they should have a Rabbi officiating at their marriage, but theoretically at least, two acceptable witnesses who are privy to a marital act and can testify to its validity, are enough to effect a marital union.

However, with regard to divorce, the situation is not so simple. The ritualistic strictures that are involved in divorce, the exacting and detailed precision which is demanded for a religious divorce, rule out many a Rabbi, even amongst the Orthodox, from being involved in divorce procedures. It takes a special type of expertise, combined with a special commitment to fulfilling the exact details of divorce legislation, to be considered reliable enough in matters of divorce. Additionally, effecting a divorce necessitates a Rabbinical tribunal, witnesses to the transmission of the divorce, and the writing of a divorce document with the proper names, date and place by a reputable and reliable scribe (called Sofer). In Jewish law, unless and until such a divorce has been delivered from husband to wife, the marriage is still intact.

Reform Rabbis, from the very outset, have scoffed at the necessity of a religious divorce. They have insisted that the civil divorce is adequate enough even as a religious base for terminating the marriage, and a couple who have received a civil divorce from the courts need not worry about failure to obtain a get and can remarry immediately. The ramifications of this attitude towards the matter of get are far reaching and in many instances quite devastating.

To fully appreciate what can unfold in the get scenario, it is important to understand the Jewish view concerning illegitimacy. Thankfully, according to Jewish law, a child born out of wedlock is not illegitimate. That is to say, if two previously unattached individuals decide to live together as cohabitates, in the absence of a Rabbinically supervised matrimonial ceremony, should they have a child, that child is not considered illegitimate by Jewish standards. What then renders a child illegitimate? Illegitimacy within Judaism can unfold either through an incestuous or an adulterous Jewish union. Thus, where there is a marriage between father and daughter or mother and son, the issue of such a marriage is illegitimate.

However, this type of scenario is not likely to unfold with great frequency. Of greater frequency is the likelihood that a child should issue from an adulterous union. By adulterous union is meant a cohabitating relationship which encroaches on an already existing union. For example, if a woman had been married, and in the course of her marriage she indulges in an affair with another man, and has a child by that other man, that child is illegitimate. Or, looking at it from the male perspective, any individual who commits adultery with an already married woman, that person's child born of such a union is illegitimate. The real question in most instances is "How can you prove that the child issues from the adulterous partner and not from the legal partner?" Truthfully, in many instances it is hard to tell, if indeed it ever becomes an issue thrust into the public arena.

On the other hand, in the situation relative to Reform divorce, the issue is more clear cut, and at the same time also much more problematic. For example, let us assume a marital union between Mr. X and Mrs. Y. Mr. X and Mrs. Y split apart after a number of years of marriage, and their Rabbi, a Reform Rabbi, wishes them luck, tells them that the civil divorce is all they need, and they can feel free to go and remarry. Mrs. Y meets a nice man, comes to her Rabbi, who is very happy that she has met a new mate, and finalizes the marriage of Mrs. Y with the new spouse Mr. Z. Mr. Z and Mrs. Y are very happy, and they have a child.

As far as Reform Judaism is concerned, it is an occasion for celebration. However, from an Orthodox point of view, this is not a cause for celebration as much as it is cause for a very disturbing problem which has been born, namely the reality that this child is illegitimate; in the popular parlance – a bastard, in the religious terminology – a mamzer. Why is the child a mamzer? Simply because Mrs. Y, in dissolving her first marriage, did not resort to the receipt of a bill of divorce called get. Instead she was satisfied with a court administered divorce. On the advice of her Rabbi, not good advice to be sure, she remarried. However, from an Orthodox point of view, she is still a married woman and now, by marrying her second husband, even with her best intentions, she is committing adultery, her union is an adulterous one, and the issue of this adulterous union reflects that adultery through the stamp of illegitimacy.

Difficult it may be, yet there are ways of getting around the conversion problem through a new conversion, however painful, however complicated, and however fraught with complexity. The matter of legitimizing illegitimates is a horse of a different color. Here one is hamstrung. The stigma of illegitimacy is very difficult to erase. But it is not merely the stigma that is a matter of the moment, it is the fact of illegitimacy. What does the fact of illegitimacy mean for the unfortunate victim, the child? It means that no one within Jewish ranks is allowed to marry that person. This, by Biblical law, is proscribed. That illegitimate person, by dint of the bad advice of the Reform Rabbi, becomes isolated and alienated from the Jewish community.

One reads in the literature of the steadily increasing rate of divorce in North American society. Whilst it is generally believed that the rate of divorce within Jewish families is not nearly as high as amongst the broader population, the impression is that it is not far behind. Given that predictions lean towards an eventual divorce rate of "one out of every two marriages;" in other words, marriage is well on the way towards becoming a true fifty-fifty proposition, the issue of religious divorce, or get, and its impact on the status of the Reform Jewish community cannot be ignored. Quite obviously, with an increasing divorce rate comes an increasing number of marriages of individuals who had previously been married and are trying once again to induce a "triumph of hope over experience." More than three-quarters of those who divorce remarry. One can easily foresee the likelihood of an increasing population of children from second marriages. Within the Reform context, this means an increasing number of illegitimate children from an Orthodox point of view.

When you add the problem of illegitimacy to the problem of conversion, the sum total is a quandary of massive proportions. We are now dealing with an ever increasing population which, for whatever reason, cannot integrate into the Orthodox community. Nor should it be assumed that this is a problem only for the Orthodox. This problem is also shared by Conservatives who lean towards tradition. Additionally, it should be stated in fairness that there is a problem with Conservative Jews of the less traditional stripe whose Rabbinic divorce is supervised by non-reliable personnel and which for all intents and purposes is equivalent to the get-less divorce of the Reform Rabbi. However, it is in Reform ranks where the problem is most acute and most prevalent, and where immediate action is necessary.

It should be noted that there is one avenue of release from the problem which has been suggested, but which has not met with unanimity. It will come as small comfort to those within Reform ranks, but it has come as welcome relief for members of Reform congregations who for some reason or other find themselves joining an Orthodox congregation, most likely because the second spouse that they meet is affiliated with an Orthodox congregation. The way out is based on the supposition that a marriage which is ministered by a Reform Rabbi may technically be considered invalid. The reasons for this are as follows. Firstly, the couple, when relying on the Reform Rabbi, place their theological eggs in the Reform Rabbi's basket and enter into the union with that Rabbi's imprimatur. However, that Rabbi's imprimatur is not one which is anchored in the Biblical tradition, and quite often is divorced from that very tradition. Many Reform Rabbis do not make use of a Hupah (wedding canopy) or Ketubah (traditional wedding contract).

The principle at work here, *Kol D'Mekadesh ada'ata D'Rabbanan Mekadesh* (whoever marries, does so via the intention of the Rabbis), makes it imperative that the marriage ceremonial comply with the Rabbinically prescribed parameters for marriage. Failing that, the marriage ceremony is questionable, and marital relations emanating from that ceremony are equally suspect.

Secondly, for the marriage to be considered legally valid, it is required that two reliable witnesses see the actual marriage ceremonial. Quite often, Reform Rabbis are in the habit of employing the parents of the bride and/or groom as witnesses in the ceremony. In Jewish tradition, this is an absolute non-starter. If anything, relatives are forbidden to serve as witnesses in matters such as this.

Thus, there is a way out which is effected through the delegitimizing of a marriage ceremony which is conducted by the Reform Rabbi. This means, in essence, that the couple were never really married according to Jewish law, that their children are as children born out of wedlock and hence, thankfully, not illegitimate, and that they therefore, ironically enough, do not need a divorce if they terminate their marriage, since they would be terminating a union which never was officially considered a legal Jewish marriage!

This is small comfort to the Reform Rabbinate, telling them that there is no problem with future illegitimacy because the marriages that they effect are not really considered valid marriages. Additionally, there are many Orthodox practitioners who are not very comfortable with this loophole. Whilst it may be true that the witnesses employed by the Reform Rabbi may not be acceptable, it is very difficult to presume that in the entire mix of guests who attend the wedding there were not two individuals who could qualify as acceptable witnesses attesting to the validity of the ceremony.

They are, willy nilly, witnesses to the marriage, which then becomes a marriage which is legally binding enough such that, upon termination, a divorce would be necessary. The legitimacy of future issue in a subsequent remarriage or cohabitate relationship is a definite problem.

Secondly, there is a prevailing view that if a couple live together as husband and wife, under the assumption that they are husband and wife, and with everyone else working under the same assumption that they are husband and wife, then it is difficult to dismiss such a union without a religious divorce called get. So, whilst the loop-hole is there, there is a reluctance, and, I might add, an underhole is there, there is a reluctance, and, I might add, an understandable reluctance, to de-legitimize all marriages conducted by Reform Rabbis. It is a double-edged sword. In actuality there is no question that the Orthodox Rabbinate does not recognize marriages effected by Reform Rabbis. On the other hand, the couple consider themselves married, and live together as husband and wife, such that there is a bindingness to their union irrelevant of who actually presided at the marriage ceremony. The couple has all the disadvantages of legally sanctioned union, with none of the advantages.

It is not the purpose of this presentation to get into the whys and the wherefores, but merely to present the issue as it is, and to put squarely on the front burner the problems that are faced in the Jewish community. The Orthodox community has very little room to maneuver in the situation. There are very strict religious qualifications for conversion and very strict religious qualifications for marriage and divorce. No Orthodox Rabbi would aggrandize to himself the right to abrogate any of these regulations. Orthodox Rabbis never see themselves as initiators of law, or as promulgaters of new regulations. Instead they see themselves as agents who have been entrusted with carrying out the law. They feel comfortable that the sanctity of life which is intrinsic to Judaism is maintained through these regulations, and there is no way that they would ever legitimize a breach.

It is one thing to be aware that breaches are taking place and to be forced to wrestle with them; it is another to resign oneself to these breaches, admit them as part and parcel of the Judaic life pattern, and stamp them with an aura of acceptablility. This is the quandary faced by the Orthodox, but it is a quandary which is quite secondary to the major issue, that issue being what lies in store for the Jewish community of tomorrow based on the problems that are proliferating today.

CHAPTER 8
CHAOS-CAN IT BE AVOIDED?

The scenario which has been painted in the previous chapters should not be dismissed as idle speculation which will never unfold. It is always difficult for individuals who are living history to actually see the flow of history, much as it is difficult for the parent who sees a child from day-to-day to actually notice the growth of the child. A stranger who visits once a year or once every two years can readily see the growth that has spread over a long term, but being close to the scene, one does not see the small movements that inch towards growth or towards destruction. It is often interesting to see historians in hindsight blame leaders or analysts for not seeing this trend or that pattern, but it takes a great degree of perception, possibly even a prophetic spirit, to be able to guage a future eventuality and to react accordingly in the present.

I do not claim for myself the gift of prophecy. I am mindful of the Talmudic remark that since the destruction of the Temple prophecy is in the hands of fools and minors. The one category I am too old to capture, the second category I would be a fool to capture! However, prophecy aside, it is possible to engage in future speculation, in predictions of what may unfold based on present patterns, and then to confront head on whatever are the ramifications of these predictions.

Based on the present policies within Reform Judaism, vis-a-vis conversion and divorce, the prospect is that the future demographic makeup of Reform Judaism will include an increasing number of non-Jews who think they are Jews, and children of questionable legitimacy who are not even aware that their legitimacy is at issue. However, from an Orthodox point of view, this matter, as well as the matter of conversion, is a pressing issue, one which cannot be ignored. Based on present trends, including the drift of Orthodoxy more and more towards the right, it is quite likely that before long, the polarization which continues to create a greater gulf between Orthodoxy and Reform will become an irreversible pattern.

The more that Reform and the Jewish population to the left of Reform become saturated with non-Jews and Jews whose ability to marry other Jews is comprised by questions of legitimacy (mamzerut), the less will the Orthodox and the traditionalists among the Conservative be involved on any interactional level with them. Reform and those to the left will evolve into a pariah-like community, a separate entity from the Orthodox. With no meaningful communication between the Orthodox and the Reform, with the two sectors diverging radically on the ever-critical social interaction level, each will go its own way – the Orthodox toward more intensive actualization of commandments, the Reform toward a new, autonomous existence. In time, marriage with a member of the Reform community may become as catastrophic for Orthodox Jews as mixed-marriage (marriage without conversion) is now. Already this is true in some Orthodox circles, and, if present trends are not altered, it can easily become a universal pattern. When this unfolds, the Jewish community will be just one step away from a calamitous divorce, with Reform detaching from the Judaic matrix and becoming a new religion. Lest the reader think this is a far-fetched potentiality, it should be noted that it would not be the first time Judaism spawned a new religion. But more about that later.

If this scenario does unfold, it will mean that Judaism will have lost 60% of its North American constituency, or somewhere close to it. The more fertile elements within Orthodoxy may eventually make up that slack, but they would be doing that anyway. They are having more children because they are fulfilling their Biblical responsibility, not in order to become more numerous than the Reform, nor for any other extraneous reason.

No matter, then, that the numbers may be replenished. Judaism simply cannot afford the tragedy of a cataclysmic divorce, the tragedy of losing 3 to 3½ million of its already relatively miniscule North American population. The trauma of such a tragedy would cut deeply into the Jewish psyche, and into the soul of every sensitive Jew. The effect such a rupture may have on every Jewish family is too overwhelming to even reduce to words. And the reverberations all across the world, in Israel, in Russia, in every community of significant Jewish salience, would be nothing short of disastrous. Those of us who think they know what an identity crisis is, either because they have been through it or have seen others go through it, have seen nothing yet. In short, we are heading for a theological, societal Civil War with no winners, only losers. Though it is the leaders of the respective trends, the Reform and Orthodox, who are the main protagonists in this unfolding drama-tragedy, it is essentially the public at large, the vast constituency of North American Jewry, which has the most to gain or lose by Rabbinic action or inaction. I emphasize Rabbinic action or inaction since it is the Rabbis who must exercise courageous leadership to avoid the future collision. If the Rabbis do not act, and with dispatch, they will have failed themselves, they will have failed their calling, and most important, they will have failed the Jews of yesterday and the Jews of tomorrow.

The first question that needs to be confronted is the matter of on whom rests the onus for this situation, and therefore the responsibility for initiating rapprochement. Undoubtedly I will be accused of working within an Orthodox bias, but whoever levels that accusation need not worry. It is not an accusation, it is a fact. Working within an Orthodox bias, I cannot help but feel that the blame for the situation, and hence the responsibility for initiating correctives, must rest with the Reform movement. After all, until Reform projected itself onto the Jewish scene, Judaism had not been monolithic, but nevertheless was guided, in matters of communal import, by Rabbinic officialdom. In fact, until Reform came on the scene, there was no Orthodox Judaism. There was Judaism, period. Orthodox Judaism was a new construct designed to differentiate traditional Judaism from those who wanted to reform it. Until Reform, Orthodoxy as we know it was the correct faith (ortho-dox) of the Jewish people.

Thus, matters of marriage and divorce as well as other legal matters were always handled by those who were acknowledged to be the experts, the scholars who had poured over Biblical law, and had explicated the Talmud – their particular specialty – over a protracted and lengthy period. The Judaism that has survived since the destruction of the Temple is primarily Talmudic Judaism. The legal constructs that remain to the present day are the halakhah which has been codified in Yosef Karo's Shulhan Arukh, and which has been further explicated by the commentaries and condensed in such volumes as Shlomo Ganzfried's abridged Code of Jewish Law. It was Reform that came upon the scene and said that Jewish norms such as divorce (get) upon dissolution of marriage, not to mention previously referred to items as the dietary regulations and Shabbat observance, are no longer necessary. Jewish mates can do without a get and just go about their business unencumbered by the need for satisfying ritualistic requirements which are deemed archaic. The Orthodox view, maintained to the present day, is that a marriage which is sanctified at its outset must be dissolved through a process of dissolution which is of a religious nature.

In the same sense as the sanctification of the Shabbat involves reciting the Kiddush, or sanctifying prayer, on Friday night, and concomitantly, a de-sanctification prayer (Havdalah) on Saturday night, a marriage, though ideally it should last forever, demands that the termination should not be simple evaporation. Instead, the parties involved should, in a religious context, dissolve the marriage through a sacred document, written in the same script as a Torah Scroll, which makes possible the re-entry of husband and wife into the marital eligibility sphere. Marriage, like the Shabbat, is sacred at both ends.

That is the philosophical justification, a rationalization, if you will, of the process. Ultimately, however, all rationalizations, however prone to argument they may be, become irrelevent, since for the Orthodox practitioner the key factor is the inescapable fact that the Bible, reinforced by the Talmud, has ordained a specific procedure for divorce which is inviolable and cannot be compromised. This is a fact of life which simply and bluntly *is*, and has been for countless generations. Orthodox Judaism will not, nor should it be expected, to change time honored traditions which are sacrosanct and which have been hallowed by continual deployment in divorce situations. Those who think they have experienced meticulousness concerning Jewish law through exacting dietary practices or Shabbat observance should see a Rabbinical court in action for a divorce. It is an eye-opener, painstaking in its resolve not to deviate one iota from prescribed procedure. There is a holiness to the divorce process which hallows all of life. To discard that process for whatever reason would be irresponsible in the extreme sense of the word.

A very strong argument can be made for the fact that Reform action and inaction in the divorce situation borders on irresponsibility, and I am frankly not sure on which side of the border. Reform cannot help but be aware of the problems they are causing by their negative attitude to Judaic norms, especially as they impact upon personal status. Whatever advantage Reform may have, in terms of allowing for religious expression amongst a group who feel uncomfortable with Orthodoxy or Conservatism and are only attracted to the type of service and practice offered by Reform, is trivial when it is measured against the damage that is done to the collective Judaic totality by the Reform attitude to such matters as divorce.

It is one thing to facilitate a population that is alienated from religious intensity; it is another to espouse and escalate Reform values into norms which are projected to be as valid as any other, and a legitimate extension of Mosaic tradition. By virtue of such vested interest protectionism, Reform has performed the greatest of disservices to its own clientele. It should be realized that the free flowing society that we live in will make it more than a rare occurence that an Orthodox family will meet a Reform family and vice versa, and that the children of such families will perhaps fall in love and desire to marry. The realization that such eventualities are quite likely is more than sufficient reason for Reform Rabbis to seriously take stock of the position they are espousing, and the damage they are causing for their own clientele, never mind the Orthodox. Also, if Reform Rabbis seriously take upon themselves the mantle of communal leadership, there is no way they can escape the communal ramifications of their policies. And those ramifications, previously elaborated, border on the disastrous (the other side of the border, to be sure). Thus, if they are to really be serious about their position of leadership in North American Jewry, Reform Rabbis have no choice but to confront this issue courageously and must be ready, willing and able to swallow crow if need be.

I am working on the assumption that the Reform Rabbinate cares. I cannot assume that they care as much as I think that they should, but if they start thinking about futuristic implications of the trends that they are setting and the problems that they are creating, they will at the very least make a first move towards resolving this issue. This is not meant to excuse away Orthodox responsibility. By claiming that the Reform must make the first move, I do not, even for a fleeting moment, exempt Orthodoxy from taking a responsible and forceful role in tackling the issues. The problems is *not* a Reform problem, it is a problem for all Jews. For the Orthodox to shirk any responsibility would be to reject one of the most crucial values, the value of *Ahavat Yisrael* (love of Israel), at a most crucial time. If Reform must make the first move, the Orthodox must be there with a receptive ear and an understanding heart.

SECTION 3
SUGGESTIONS

CHAPTER 9
A DIVORCE PROPOSAL

Insofar as divorce is concerned, the first move that Reform needs to make is to *rethink* its policy of not necessitating a religious bill of divorce at the time of marriage collapse. By using the word "rethink" I am indulging in euphemism. I really mean by this that they should adopt the policy that a religiously sanctioned marriage, no matter by whom, should be dissolved only via a religious divorce, before any remarriage occurs. The question is, "Who will supervise the divorce?" True enough, the mere adoption of the idea that divorce by religious fiat is required is a very significant step, but significant as it is, this is not a sufficient step. A religious divorce which does not meet the halakhic guidelines is, for all intents and purposes, equivalent to no get at all. A sufficient step would be to introduce a system whereby divorce is handled through an official and universally recognized Rabbinic court that would service the entire Jewish community.

This is not to be taken in the form of an official proposal representing any specific group, but it is perhaps a point of departure for resolution of this dilemma. The structure that would be created in addressing this issue could also function for the other volatile issue presently under discussion, conversion. It is obvious that egos are involved in this situation, and it is unrealistic to suppose that the Reform Rabbinate will totally abdicate on its conceived right to make pronouncements concerning matters such as divorce and conversion. Therefore, it would be useful and advisable to create an umbrella organization incorporating the trends within the American Rabbinical spectrum. This umbrella organization would be the facilitating, administrative *clearing house* for matters of personal status. It would be a form of referral agency which would channel all requests for divorce and conversion coming from Orthodox, Conservative, Reform, and "other" Rabbis. The actual divorce or conversion itself, and the administration of the halakhic (Judeo legal) aspects of the divorce or conversion would be solely in the hands of the halakhic experts, admittedly primarily Orthodox sages who would be the Rabbinical court for this matter.

The advantages of such a setup are immediately apparent. All divorces would conform to the *halakhah* (Jewish law), and all marital separations would be followed by a halakhically sanctioned divorce. This would avoid any problems down the road of families having to worry that a divorce is not recognized and the legitimacy of their progeny is in question. The actual handling of the divorce itself would be done by universally recognized Rabbinic authorities who would form a Beth Din, a Rabbinical Court which should have no problem being accepted by the global Jewish community. Any difficulties that may accrue from Reform or Conservative involvement in this arrangement would be avoided via the Beth Din being totally independent in terms of halakhic function. However, at the same time this Rabbinic court would be at the call of all the Rabbinic organizations, whom they would agree to serve in their capacity as experts on handling divorce. The actual coming together of Orthodox, Conservative and Reform Rabbis, not to speak of the agreement of the Orthodox and Reform Rabbinate to such a plan, is not an easy matter, but intense pressure, prodded by the realization that failure to make a move such as this will eventually lead to chaos, may carry the day. The Jewish public has heretofore not really been aware of the volcanic eruption that is presently simmering under the Jewish community. Setting off a *public* clamor for action, for applied pressure on Jewish leadership to act with immediacy, is a necessary part of the process of problem resolution. The "Theological Clearing House" is just one proposal among others that may be suggested in the desire to sincerely confront the issues.

Admittedly, in the past, the Orthodox Rabbinate in general, and to be more precise, the right wing element within Orthodoxy, has been reluctant to get together with Conservative and Reform representatives on any issue. One well remembers the controversy which arose almost two decades ago concerning the matter of Orthodox representation in the umbrella organization known as the Synagogue Council of America. There were verbally violent protestations against the Union of Orthodox Jewish Congregations and the Rabbinical Council of America joining in this broad-based group, which also has under its umbrella the Conservative and Reform Rabbinic and Synagogue organizations. That debate has been resurrected in the past few years, partly as a result of the increasing movement towards the right that is carrying the day in Orthodoxy. Nevertheless, the Rabbinical Council of America, the most representative Orthodox Rabbinic body in North America, and the Union of Orthodox Jewish Congregations of America, the biggest organization representing Orthodox Synagogues in North America, continue to be counted amongst the groups that place themselves under the Synagogue Council of America umbrella.

Again, there is a difference between the Synagogue Council of America and the organization herein being proposed. The Synagogue Council of America is not an halakhic body, and is specifically enjoined from making pronouncements regarding Jewish law. It was on this understanding that the Orthodox organizations entered the Synagogue Council in the first place. Were there any question that by entering the Synagogue Council they would be compromising Jewish law, these organizations would never have entered, and if that reality changes today, they would opt out, or at least the pressures to opt out would be so intense that they would be almost impossible to resist.

The theological clearing house proposal herein suggested is a little more than just an umbrella body for political clout and social action, which the Synagogue Council is in the main. The clearing house would definitely have some relationship to the halakhic process, although it would not be directly involved in it. It is a touchy issue and I do not propose to place my head into the theological chopping block on this, but the dangers that rear themselves from failure to come up with a workable solution for this problem are too massive for any responsible Rabbinate to ignore. The Orthodox Rabbinate will have to seriously question its own feeling that participation implies recognition, that by participating with the Reform they will be lending theological credibility to the Reform movement. This type of an attitude will foreclose any possibility of working together with a significant and vital element of the Judaic spectrum towards problem resolution.

Of course, it would be easy for the Orthodox to go to sleep at night and say that it is not the fault of the Orthodox, it is the Reform that have caused the problem and it is they who must come full circle and divest themselves from all involvement, however remote, in the halakhic process, whilst at the same time acknowledging halakhah's primacy. Even assuming that this feeling may have a fool-proof logic of its own, it is nevertheless the case that at this point in time such a move by Reform is highly unlikely to unfold. And, in the context of not compromising any iota of the halakhah, there is room to maneuver, to stretch out a welcome mat to the Reform so that they feel part and parcel of ultimate Jewish destiny, and work together with the Orthodox and Conservatives towards a viable alternative to disarray, chaos, and ultimate disintegration.

One of the key issues involved in this new theological clearing house, assuming that it is acceptable and accepted by the various Rabbinic groups, is the question of retroactivity. There are undoubtedly those within Reform who, if they take this proposal seriously, would be willing to come to the bargaining table ready to talk about the future if the Orthodox will guarantee that all those who have gone through Reform procedures in the past are not hassled, and are deemed by the Rabbinic tribunal to be okay. If this is a sine qua non for entry into this common undertaking, then again we have a stumbling block which could become an impenetrable obstruction. No Orthodox Rabbi, no Rabbi has the right to abrogate items of halakhah, either in retrospect or in prospect. By abdicating on the need for a halakhically valid *get* for those who were divorced prior to the implementation of this clearing house, Rabbis would in effect be saying that Biblical law has been suspended and in a hundred instances or even in one instance, has been rendered non-operative. By so doing, however, they open the possibility that this will happen again in the future. But more than that, they compromise the bindingness of the halakhic process by saying that there are execeptions; but there are no exceptions since any exceptions break the rule. Thus, this type of bargaining may be good for unions in salary disputes, but is not possible in matters of halakhic import. The law is God given, and even God, from the traditional perspective, cannot now make changes to the law. The law, the Torah, is God's law given to human beings as trustees. Trustees have a mandate to carry out, they do not have a mandate to destroy or to misrepresent.

The outsider, observing the scenario that is unfolding in this issue, may ask the following question – based on the assumption that in all negotiations there is give and take on both sides, it seems that here the Orthodox are doing all the taking and none of the giving. In what inheres the fairness of this negotiating process? Well, in fact it may not seem as if the Orthodox are giving anything, but this is not the case. True, on the one hand the Reform would be admitting the concept of get (religious divorce) into its framework, and would then steer their congregants towards accepting an halakhic bill of divorce via the theological clearing house. This, for the Reform, is a radical about face. Additionally, they would do the same with all those who in the past have been told by their Reform Rabbis that a get was not necessary. The Reform would now be turning around, swallowing crow if you will, and admitting to those whom they had previously advised one way, that there is a new reality and it is proper that they seek a religious divorce.

By the way, as uncomfortable as it may presently seem, if rapprochement can be effected, it should not be too difficult or uncomfortable for Reform Rabbis to explain the far reaching significance of their new policy, and the importance of total participation by all Jews of whatever stripe.

The Reform, then, are making all the concessions, and the Orthodox are making absolutely no concessions. But that is not the way negotiations are supposed to work.

At the very outset, the Orthodox are likely to claim that they really should not feel obliged to make any concessions since they cannot concede in matters of halakhah and besides, it was not they who broke away from halakhah and therefore it is not incumbent upon them to make any concessions. However, aside from this argumentation, which would hopefully only be an initial resistance, it should not be forgotten that the Orthodox would be making a very significant concession, namely that they would be working together with the Reform. This means that they would participate with the Reform, thus acknowledging Reform as a force to be reckoned with, although at the same time they would not in any way concede one millimeter of halakhic ground in their working together with Reform. But the fact that they would sit together with Reform and work together with them would be, from an Orthodox vantage point, a very major adjustment of thinking.

This may not seem tangibly significant in any way to the skeptic, but should not be down-played. It is without historical precedent for those who represent tradition to give any form of credibility, even if that credibility is not in the form of theological recognition, to a group which from a religious perspective is considered a pack of heretics, scoffers, perhaps even blasphemers. If it is that bad, then how can it even be expected that the Orthodox will make this adjustment? Not readily, and not easily, but perhaps the farsighted leadership within Orthodoxy will seize the moment and see this as an instance of "A moment to act on God's behalf," and will suspend temporarily one of its fundamental principals in the interests of the ultimate survival of the Jewish Community.

Additionally, there may be other avenues via which Orthodoxy can make what would be seen as significant gestures, although they would not necessarily compromise religious law. One relates to the aforementioned loophole of invalidating marriages that were performed by Reform Rabbis because they did not satisfy the religious requirements. The issue of retroactivity certainly can not be washed away with a carte blanche nullification of halakhic law for past cases. Instead, each individual case would have to be referred to the theological clearing house and, through the theological clearing house, to its Rabbinical Beth Din for adjudication.

However, were this Rabbinic body to employ the loophole of non-recognition of prior marriages officiated at solely by Reform Rabbis, it would go a long way towards solving the backlog problem, and also towards avoiding problems of legitimacy based on the failure of many families in the past to obtain a get. What the guidelines would be for when this loophole could be employed and when it could not is a technical matter than need not be further discussed here, although it should be said that it would be much easier to employ such a loophole when the marriage took place in a small group of family only, such that the possibility that there were acceptable witnesses to the ceremony are reduced to zero.

Then again, the fact that we would in many instances be dealing with emergencies, in that the couples have already been married and have children from the new marriages, would make for a "b'dee'avad" (after the fact) situation where halakhah is always more lenient than in a "Lekhatchila" (before the fact) situation. Where there has not yet been a subsequent marriage, or where there has been a subsquent marriage but there have been no children, it is quite likely that the Rabbinic tribunal would insist on a divorce to obviate all future problems.

There is another, more technical avenue that may be contemplated in this period of exigency. It is the possibility of retroactively annulling a marriage, which may be achieved if the husband, in the spirit of cooperation, would appoint a proxy to de-liver a bill of divorce (get) to his former wife and then would cancel that very proxy other than in the presence of the appointed agent. Whether and how this loophole applies has been a matter of intense debate in halakhic circles, and it must be left for the scholars to explicate this issue. It should be noted that from time immemorial, the sages worked with the principle that there is no obligation to increase the number of mamzerim (illegitimates) and, on the contrary, we have an obligation to decrease that number.

In any event, we would be dealing with a manageable situation if for no other reason than that everyone would be gathered together with a view towards cooperation and solving problems rather creating them. It would work with the confidence that there is good will on the part of all concerned, and that the halakhah has sufficient wherewithall for tackling some of the problems involved. Surely they cannot undo all the damage, but at least an honest attempt to partially redress the situation should be possible. And in the main, by redressing, they will have effectively blunted a much more serious crisis that would have surely unfolded in the ensuing generations.

Before tackling the more delicate matter of conversion in this theological clearing house, it should be noted that there is one element in this entire proposal that has not been discussed, but which is highly relevant although hopefully not a particularly nagging sore. This is the ubiquitous problem of "How much will it cost?" To begin this discussion, I would say categorically that no matter how much it will cost, it is well worth the price. What we are really asking is what price are we willing to pay to prevent disintegration within a very significant element of the Jewish community in the course of the next few decades. Since we work with the assumption that every Jewish person is of infinite value, we really cannot put a price tag on life, on infinite value, and certainly not on the value of a community, a community being the conglomerate of individuals of infinite value.

Having said that, it should be understood that what we are talking about here is a massive undertaking which will necessitate a main office and branch offices that are spread out in various locales in the United States and Canada, verily in every place where there is a concentrated Jewish community. There is no city in the United States or Canada with a significant Jewish community which does not have the problems that have been discussed herein. And therefore, only by having such offshoots of the main clearing house in all these cities will every Jewish family have the opportunity to take care of their particular religious dilemmas.

If the rate of divorce is anywhere near what has been suggested in the literature, then we are talking about thousands upon thousands of Jewish families that are in need of religious bills of divorce. This is a backlog of herculean dimensions which will necessitate the creation of a massive organization to adequately tackle these situations. It will demand an increasing number of scribes to write divorces, an increasing number of Rabbinic experts to administer the divorces, and full time staff to arrange appointments, prepare documents, and see through other related matters. It is a job that will take years to implement, and years to provide the proper personnel to make sure that this problem is adequately covered.

But where the need arises, the Jewish community has been able in the past to come up with adequate resources to meet those needs. For example, the demand for kosher meat in North America is significantly higher today than it has ever been, what with a greater Jewish population in North America, and what with a greater number adhering to kashruth regulations, a greater number of hotels offering kosher food, and a greater number of affairs which demand kosher cuisine. This means that the Jewish community has been forced to provide a greater number of Shochtim (ritual slaughterers), so that the demand can be met. And with a greater number of slaughterers has come the need for a greater and more comprehensive supervisory body, or as has been the case in the matter of kosher food, many supervisory bodies. They all serve a purpose because they provide services that are desperately needed.

We will be forced to establish a learning institution to train scribes who would be able to handle the heavy volume of divorces. Like the kashruth situation, demand would create supply. More scribes could be of immense usefulness to the North American Jewish population, for, aside from writing divorces, they could also in their spare time write the parchments for the phylacteries (tefilin) and mezuzot. These items have become increasingly costly in the past decade, and an ample supply of proper parchments is sure to impact positively on the affordability factor.

I retain the confidence that if all the Rabbinic groups are fully cognizant of the emergency proportions of the issue, and impress this upon their respective clientele, they will receive the financial support that is necessary to properly tackle this issue. And their working together in a common cause will undoubtedly do wonders in terms of awakening a Judaic consciousness that has heretofore been dormant amongst many in the North American Jewish population. The expense will be great, but the rewards will more than justify any expense that will be incurred.

There has been much talk about the need to establish a "Sefer Yuchsin" (Book of Geneological Pedigree) for the North American Jewish community. That talk has come from the right, ever-cognizant of the pedigree problems arising from increasing divorce and conversion not carried out in accordance with Jewish law. Such a Book of Geneological Pedigree tends toward exclusivity, towards establishing those whose geneological credentials are impeccable and thus pose no problems for marriage. The theological clearing house could serve the same purpose, but its purpose would be inclusivistic – to include as many Jews as possible, ideally the close to 6,000,000 Jews of North America, in the big list of who is, without a doubt, part of the Jewish community.

CHAPTER 10
A CONVERSION PROPOSAL

In war, the order of one general can move an entire army. In peace, especially in a democracy, it is almost impossible to move an entire people. However, were the Rabbinical hierarchy of each sector within Judaism unbending in its resolve, the direction that it would give to Rabbis within the respective constituencies, and the direction that the Rabbis themselves would give to the members of their congregations, could make for a collective effort, in unanimity, somewhat akin to a general in an army situation. Policy changes can make for overwhelming shifts in direction, and in this instance can make for a significant contribution to a dynamic equilibrium in the Jewish community.

The matter of a common front for conversion is not as easily reconciled, even in the mere proposition for a solution, as the matter of divorce. The divorce situation is slightly more facile since until the present time, Reform has in the main not been involved with ritual divorce. It is thus relatively easy to make a quantum leap into divorce as it presently exists, which is primarily an Orthodox specialty, although there are some Conservative practitioners who do engage in divorce; and also some within the Conservative ranks whose expertise in divorce is questionable, and whose practices with regard to divorce are even more questionable.

In conversion, however, Reform is in up to its neck. The highest number of conversions are undoubtedly done by the Reform, and if it is to be believed that approximately ten thousand conversions are finalized each year in North America, the lion's share are in the Reform matrix. By what stretch of the concept of compromise, or accommodation, to use a more precise terminology, can a bridge be built between the polar opposites of the Orthodox attitude to conversion, which is essentially a reflection of Orthodox belief and practice, and Reform conversion, which is equally a reflection of Reform belief and practice?

The proposal concerning conversion essentially works along the same structural guidelines as the proposal for divorce. That is to say, that the theological clearing house which would have administrative responsibilities to steer all divorce problems to an autonomously functioning Rabbinical court, would do the same with conversions. However, with conversions the issue is a little bit more complicated. Any conversion that is worth its salt must be preceded by an educational process. But, who are to be the educators?

Obviously, from an Orthodox point of view, teaching a prospective convert that the dietary laws are not important and non-essential is a fundamental contravention of a primary requirement of conversion – that the convert knows of basic Jewish norms, and promises to adhere to them upon becoming a Jew. Obviously then, the Orthodox could not countenance having instructors as official teachers for the Rabbinical tribunal unless these teachers can educate in the ways of tradition, which is a euphemism for the teachers themselves being traditional, else they would be poor teachers of that which they have renounced or do not put into practice. The duplicity, the hypocrisy of such teaching is pedagogically unsound, and the fraud easily picked up by any semi-astute prospective convert.

On the other hand, it is at the same time logical to assume that no self-respecting Reform Rabbi would be able to function in a situation where he would be obliged to send prospective converts to an educational setting where in effect the convert is expected to adopt an Orthodox lifestyle, or a holier-than-them affirmation of Judaism. We would then be asking the Reform to cut off their collective noses to spite their basic ideology. Undoubtedly, this is something that the Orthodox would like to do, and would certainly welcome the opportunity to destroy the foundations of Reform as an entrenched theological system. However, since we are dealing with an issue which must be resolved practically, and at the same time not involve halakhic compromise, it is beyond the pale of imagination to even contemplate that Reform would go so far as to agree that all conversions from now on be affirmations of Orthodox ideology; and this is, even before we contemplate the question of what to do with those who have already undergone Reform conversions.

Prior to addressing the question of the modus operandi for possible accommodation in this very sensitive and delicate matter, it should be noted that the Orthodox Rabbinate has been very reluctant to confront the question of conversion with any strong semblance of responsibleness. The overwhelming majority of Orthodox Rabbis freely and unabashedly say, even with a sense of pride, that they do not handle any conversions. It is often left to a few individuals to carry and shoulder the burden of this ever expanding problem, and who by so doing must do the work of many, many Rabbis. Beware of conversion burnout.

Then there are some Orthodox Rabbis who grudgingly take a handful of conversions, and these only if they measure up to the scrupulous standards that are set by the Rabbi. Experience has shown, however, that the end result, on a broad statistical basis, is approximately the same whether the Rabbi's standards are exacting in terms of the number that he takes, or the Rabbi is more accommodating in this regard. The number of conversions which become reversions, or movements back to theological limbo, are probably the same no matter what are the standards of the officiating Rabbinical court.

The Orthodox Rabbinate in general has also been reluctant to have what are known as conversion classes. This stems from a reluctance to institutionalize the notion of conversion. Instead, each conversion is taken on an individual basis, as a reaction to a problem. To formalize the approach is to welcome prospects. But precisely because the Orthodox Rabbinate would prefer to look the other way insofar as conversions are concerned, there is reluctance to implement anything definitive. It is a question of reacting rather than acting. On the other hand, Conservative Rabbis, and to a larger extent Reform Rabbis, have been much more open with regard to conversions. That openness is manifested firstly in terms of not being reluctant to handle conversions, and secondly in terms of having classes as well as programs for the prospective converts and outreach programs following the conversion itself.

I mention this disparity in approach merely to press home the idea that even the thought of setting up a Rabbinical court with branches all over North America to deal with the processing of conversions, involves for the Orthodox a fundamental change in attitude. There is no guarantee that this can happen with rapidity, even if it can happen at all. If it does happen, it will only be after an avalanche of weighty and responsible opinion projecting the importance of having such Rabbinic tribunals in order to obviate an alternative which is far worse, namely assimilation and the potential loss of hundred of thousands, if not millions of Jews.

Now to the matter of the modus operandi. There are tangible aspects to the conversion process, and intangible aspects. The tangible aspects are, for the male, ritual circumcision or, if medical circumcision has already been done, covenental letting of blood, followed by immersion in the ritual bath called mikvah; and, for the woman, the tangible aspect of conversion is the immersion in the mikvah. The intangible aspect of conversion is the acceptance of the commandments, the commitment to adhere to the corpus of Jewish ritual and ethical practice, what is referred to in the parlance as "kabalat hamitzvot."

With regard to the issue of circumcision, there are really no halfway measures. Either we adopt the imperative to place a covenental imprint on the organ which generates posterity, or we do not. Halfway measures, or half a circumcision, are non-starters. Needless to say, here, as in other instances, there is no way that the tradition, the fulfillment of the Biblical precept requiring circumcision, can be compromised. This effectively means that for the sake of community coherence, the Reform would be obliged to go along with having all their prospective male converts circumcised, or, if they have already been medically circumcised, having them enter into the covenant via a token blood letting (hatafat dam brit).

The matter of immersion in the ritual bath, or mikvah, follows along the same lines as the matter of ritual circumcision. Here it is an across-the-board requirement of both male and female converts. Again, the immersion in the mikvah, and its being attested to by the Rabbinical tribunal, is an item which cannot be compromised. There are many within Reform who see the entire institution of mikvah as being archaic, and especially recoil at the requirement that females enter into the mikvah in their birthday suits and in the presence of three Rabbis. Just the thought of having to go through this is enough to scare away even the most sincere convert. However, the converting female should be aware that it is not as bad as it sounds. There are various methodologies which can be engaged in, such that the convert can be below water before the Rabbis take a quick look just to make sure that there has been a total immersion. In such an instance, the Rabbis actually see no flesh, so that the dignity of the person immersing is maintained.

There are already some Reform Rabbis who, in a gesture which to them is more than mere tokenism, but which from an Orthodox point of view still leaves halakhic gaps, actually take their prospective converts to the mikvah. Making mikvah immersion a requirement of conversion is another hard pill for Reform to swallow, but there is no way around this if we are actually to resolve the major issues discussed herein. Presently, there are some cities where those who are responsible for the community mikvah actually do not allow Reform the use of the mikvah. The reasoning is that by allowing Reform to use the mikvah, either the conversion is mistakenly assumed to be endorsed by the community, or the Reform and the converts are left with the impression that the conversion is valid even by Orthodox standards, since, after all, there was a ritual immersion. There are, then, obvious and not so obvious points of friction, which a common assault by communal leaders may alleviate.

It is left now to discuss the tricky item referred to as acceptance of the commandments, or "kabalat hamitzvot." As mentioned previously, this, unlike circumcision and mikvah immersion, is an intangible. The reasons why this is an intangible will become clear as it is further elaborated. If one would take the strictest Orthodox interpretation of kabalat hamitzvot, it means that the convert would be required to study the basic commandments which characterize Jewish law in all their particulars, and then, after having studied these, accept, in sincerity and with firm conviction, the philosophical roots and underpinnings of the faith and the commandments, as well as the commitment to actualize these commandments on a regular basis, without fail, without compromise, without deviation.

The prospective convert almost always wonders why he or she is expected to be more observant than the mainstream Jew, who even if espousing some form of Orthodox practice, is still likely to deviate here and there, or to show human frailties in terms of catering to self-serving desires at the expense of certain mitzvah fulfillments. Why then should the convert be required to go one better?

76

The classic answer that is offered to this question is the one which relates to the matter of citizenship in a country. One who is born in the United States or Canada automatically becomes a citizen of that country. However, one who is born outside the United States or Canada, and desires to go through the process of naturalization, will be obliged, at some point in time, to swear allegiance to the host country. One who is born in the United States or Canada, by virtue of that fortunate stroke of fate, will not be compelled, at any point in time, to declare allegiance to the country of birth, and would then harbor no guilt feelings for having sworn to be true to the rules and regulations of the country and then having become a scofflaw, a common thief, or what not.

However, one who is naturalized, and who has obviously joined the United States or Canada in free choice, probably has a greater appreciation of all the advantages that the host country offers. At the same time, such an individual sees so many who were born in their country taking advantage of the country and not really appreciating it to the full, yet the outsider will be required to take an oath. The outsider will have no choice but to make a statement obligating the self to be a good citizen, something that many others are not.

This is taken as a natural component of the process of entry into a new system. It speaks of the very fundamental notion that those who are entering into a new context, be it a new country, or a new faith, or a new fraternity, must do so on the terms of that country, that faith, that fraternity or sorority. They cannot come in and say that they will maintain their own independent thinking but just want the advantages that are offered by the host country, the faith, the fraternity or the sorority. Any country, faith, or fraternity that allows membership based on such cavalier attitudes, invites disaster. If you cannot impress the importance of allegiance prior to entry, it is quite unlikely that allegiance will be forthcoming at any later stage.

This applies in understandable fashion to conversion to Judaism. It goes without saying that, as in the situation of citizens of the United States and Canada, there are those who by accident of birth are Jewish by definition, but who scoff at it, take advantage of it, and do not at all appreciate the beauty of Jewish tradition. On the other hand, those who have made a free-willed decision to enter into the Jewish mainstream have ostensibly found a kinship with the Jewish faith and the Jewish lifestyle. For them, Judaism is something to be cherished and appreciated. Indeed, there are many would-be converts; there are also many need-be reverts.

In this regard, it should be noted that there is hardly any difference between Orthodox, Conservative and Reform Judaism. If one for the moment suspends the differences that exist between the Orthodox, Conservative, and Reform sectors, one commonality is shared by all of these ideologies. They insist that the

convert who enters into the Judaic fold adopt either the Orthodox, Conservative, or Reform notion of faith and practice. In the
Orthodox context it is a much more demanding commitment,
within the Conservative, less so, and within the Reform, quite
liberal, but nevertheless there is an across-the-board understanding that there are some basic norms that need to be adhered
to, which are uncompromisable, and which clearly define what is
meant by entry into the Judaic covenantal community.

Even if one adopts the most stringent of views with regard to
conversion, namely that one must be totally aware of all the commandments, even all the nuances within the commandments, and
accept these as one's lifestyle, it is quite obvious that this is a pie-
in-the-sky ideal that can hardly be realized in actual practice. We
would in effect totally block out the entire possibility of conversion if we insisted that before the prospective convert joined the
Jewish community, he or she knew everything and accepted everything. To know everything is an almost impossible task that has
not been realized by the greatest of sages. Certainly one cannot
realistically expect that the convert, even before immersion,
should transcend the scholarly achievements of the greatest sages
in Israel.

Therefore, realistically, we must be dealing with a more sober
and prudent attitude. The convert is obliged to know the basic
faith, the basic norms, the basic traditions, and the basic nuances
within those traditions, but for the convert to be expected to
know every single detail of every single observance is to eliminate
the possibility of conversion at the starting gate. For example, it
would be expected that the convert should know the importance
of ritual circumcision, the importance of this symbolizing a covenantal bond between the human being and God. However, I
doubt whether any Rabbi would ask that the convert know what
level of bilirubin cannot, under normal circumstances, be ex-
ceeded if a child is to have the circumcision on the eighth day.
Similarly, with regard to essential items such as the observance of
Shabbat, the maintaining of the dietary regulations, or the observance of the rules of family life, undoubtedly the broad conceptions concerning these observances must be part and parcel of
the convert's vocabulary, but to insist that the convert know by
heart every single one of the thirty nine categories of work pro-
hibited on the Shabbat and some of the emanations from these
categories, is to insist on a mastery of detail which goes beyond
the basic requirements as spelled out in the codes.

It seems, from the codes, that conversion works, to a certain
extent, along the lines of the "negation of negation." That is to
say, the convert must affirm allegiance to Jewish faith and Jewish
practice, and, if the convert is to be accepted, must not negate
any of the commandments or any of the nuances within the commandments. If the convert says, "I will adhere to everything except that I cannot ruin my house by knocking holes into the door

post to affix a mezuzah nor will I compromise the paint by pasting it, and therefore I must have a house without the proper mezuzah attached to the door posts," then that convert is dismissed.

If per chance, however, the education of the convert missed a certain mitzvah which, if the convert had learned of it, he or she would have had trouble with it, and the convert learns of this only many years down the road, there is little evidence that this compromises the original conversion, and every evidence that it does not. In other words, and based on the primary sources concerning conversion, the convert is made aware of the basic categories of observance and then, if the convert is willing to accept the responsibility to observe these commandments and the entire corpus of Jewish law, the convert is readily accepted.

It is precisely in this that the intangible quality of kabalat hamitzvot inheres. Depending on who the teacher is, the scope of knowledge that is imparted to the convert can vary greatly, even if we are dealing only with Orthodox Rabbis. Additionally, the time requirement for legitimate conversion varies from Rabbi to Rabbi.

I have been told of Rabbis of yesteryear, reliable Orthodox Rabbis, who would indulge in the following scenario. The Jewish male and his non-Jewish prospective convert and spouse would meet in the morning with the Rabbi and his wife, the Rabbi's wife would instruct the woman in the morning, take her to the ritual immersion in the afternoon, and then the Rabbi would marry the couple in the evening. Whilst one recoils from engaging in such a process today, there is room for argument that this procedure did not contravene basic Jewish law.

Jewish law does not in any way suggest a mandatory waiting period prior to conversion. In the absence of a supportive Jewish community which actually lives out Jewish norms to the full, and with the challenges of an open society where reversion is increasingly likely, the Rabbinic insistence on planting firmer roots before taking the plunge is well founded. But this should not be seen as an halakhic requirement per se, as much as a perceptive application of the desires of Jewish law to the present contingencies. There is thus one area which, by virtue of its being a value judgment, is a matter that could be open to further scrutiny in trying to find accommodation in the conversion dilemma.

With regard to the more substantive issue of observance itself, there is a great dichotomy between what is meant by observance in Orthodox tradition and what is meant by observance in Reform tradition. From what has been discussed herein, one finds it difficult to even talk in terms of mandatory Reform observance. The basic ideology of Reform is loose by definition, since it is deemed as contrary to the Reform ethos to codify imperatives, to set down do's and don'ts. There are nice options, but very little requirements. This being the case, how does one bridge the vast gap between lack of any observance requirements on the Reform side, and insistence on observance on the Orthodox side?

I do not claim to possess any magical solutions to this problem. Obviously the great minds who pore over the minutae of Jewish law will have to apply themselves to this problem in a spirit of understanding, whilst weighing fully the possible consequences of lenient or strict interpretations. If there is room for flexibility, it would be in the way one interprets the notion of acceptance of the commandments. Since it is not required that the convert learn all of the nuances with regard to the specific command-ments, but rather must evoke a general philosophical and practical acceptance of the commandments, there *may be*, and I accent the words *may be*, room for contemplating the possibility that a loose affirmation of allegiance to the concepts underlining the pre-cepts may be a minimal standard which could be employed in some instances.

Also, demanding the convert's assurance that the command-ments will be observed is a complicated construct. Which Rab-binical court can guarantee that the convert will keep the com-mandments? The rabbinical court is under no constraint to de-liver fool-proof guarantees, only to have a sincere undertaking by the convert, a commitment that is authentic, free of chicanery. This, too, is obviously a relatively loose frame of reference, allow-ing for interpretations ranging from rigid to accommodating. This range is well within halakhic parameters.

It should be recognized that there are great dangers and stumbl-ing blocks in opening up such avenues to conversion. It would be very difficult for the Orthodox community to, at one and the same time, insist on one set of standards for Orthodox conver-sions, and then employ a different set of standards for the theo-logical clearing house. Yet, there is the flip side to this reality, and that is the critical issue of the need to maintain the community as a whole, and to forestall the possibility of massive defections. Whilst the idea of maintaining communal unity is a very vital concept, it need not be done at the price of abrogating any regula-tion or halakhah within Judaism. However, where a lenient view or interpretation within the matrix of halakhah is possible, the added component of maintaining communal coherence makes such a lenient interpretation desirable, if not mandatory.

It should be noted that responsible and respected sages have argued that even if the prospective convert gives no indication of expecting to observe the commandments, it is still a mitzvah (religious fulfillment), I repeat, a *mitzvah* to accept such a convert! The argument that we should close the door on conversions since the overwhelming majority of converts do not observe the com-mandments even for a brief period, is met with the counter-argu-ment that it is a mitzvah to accept converts. And, additionally, closing the door on conversion forces the convert and the Jewish partner out of the Jewish fold, possibly even to another religion.

Adopting a closed-door policy could evolve into a tragedy of immense proportions, given the high and ever increasing number of Jews who are "seriously socializing" with non-Jews.

Should the Orthodox community actually decide in favour of an accommodating posture, it would be a tremendous gesture of good will, based on a very significant change in attitude. It should convince even the greatest skeptic of the seriousness with which the Orthodox view the future of the North American Jewish community. Even more so than in the issue of divorce, where it can be argued that the Orthodox concession is merely a tokenism which is not really substantive, here in conversion this is not the case.

There are those who may think that what is being proposed is heresy, or at the very least an argument for abdication of the halakhah. This is certainly not true. Instead, what is being suggested is that the halakhah be searched out very carefully to see what room for maneuverability is left open.

The theological clearing house concept, if adopted for conversion, would be based on an agreement between the leadership of all sectors in Jewish religious life regarding the need for circumcision, ritual immersion, and acceptance of the commandments (kabalat hamitzvot) in some universally workable fashion, for all prospective converts. All Rabbis would refer their candidates to the clearing house, which would supply the proper instruction or arrange that proper instruction be given. The teachers, much like the scribes for divorce, would be specialists with precise pedagogical skills in approaching the delicate matter of conversion. The finalization of conversion could easily be done in the presence of the referring Rabbi, but attested to only by the Rabbinical court that services the clearing house. This avoids all problems concerning who is eligible or disqualified from serving as judge in this matter. And, coming from the top, so to say, and thus fully recognized, Denver-type debacles would be avoided.

Let it be recognized that up until the present moment, the tendency within Orthodox ranks is to take a maximalist approach to conversion requirements. One can understand the motivations for such policy. The Orthodox community desires to maintain its Orthodoxy, and at the same time to allow entry into Judaism only to those who profess to authentic Orthodox practice. This being the case, the standards that the Orthodox set for converts are the same standards that they would theoretically set for any Jew who would ask the question, "what should I observe on a regular basis in order to conform with my responsibility as a Jew?"

However, in the context of the broader community, and in placing upon Orthodoxy the burden for making decisions not only for the Orthodox, but for the entire North American Jewish community, the Orthodox Rabbinical hierarchy has a responsibility to transcend their previous position, to look at the greater realities and how Orthodoxy can accommodate these realities. Whatever halakhic categories are employed in confronting the issues, one mitzvah must not be ignored, the mitzvah to preserve the Jewish community.

Concerning conversion as well as divorce, although the solution need not be available tomorrow, the process of being vitally concerned with coming up with solutions should be launched with immediacy. Only then is there a reasonable hope that the Orthodox community, indeed the entire Jewish community, will be ready before the crunch comes, and ideally, will be able to ward off the crunch. Even if solutions can be found for the divorce problem, but not for the conversion problem, or vice versa, I would argue that half a solution is a solution to a major component of the overall problem, and much better than nothing. Failing that, the prospect of societal chaos within the North American Jewish community and its resultant fallout cannot be ruled out.

In the next chapter, I will try to project the dark-side scenario in its proper historical perspective. Hopefully, when the awareness of this eventuality takes root, solutions such as those proposed herein will be placed on the front burner of Jewish priorities. For once, the Jewish community has a chance to act rather than to react, to anticipate a problem rather than to indulge in crisis management, a type of management which always has a short fall in efficiency, because of the disadvantages of working under pressure or in the volatility of desperation.

CHAPTER 11
CAN IT HAPPEN? AGAIN?

Undoubtedly, even after having explained how the future cataclysm can unfold, there are many who will remain skeptical about this venture into futurology. Can it really happen? That is the question, although it is technically not a precise question. The precise question is, can it happen again? Why again? Because it has already happened once before.

Before examining the question of can it happen, it would be useful to place this futuristic question into historical perspective. Reform was not the first instance of a movement established in opposition to the Rabbis, as an anti-Rabbinism movement. Prior to Reform, there were many such movements of differing sizes and with differing impacts.

In the 18th century, the Hasidic movement began, through the inspiration of Rabbi Israel Baal Shem Tov, popularly known as the Besht. For a long time, Hasidism distinguished itself from the Mitnagdim, those who opposed the Hasidic movement, by saying that the Mitnagdim were fearful of sinning against the law, but the Hasidim were fearful of sinning against God. The hasidic movement began as a populist movement, designed to attract the masses of Jews who were outside the pale and beyond the reach of the Rabbis, with their emphasis on intensive study. It was a grass roots movement, geared to take the alienated, disaffected Jews who could not relate to the intellectual intrigue of the Rabbis, and bring them back into the fold through affirming the holiness and the sanctity of each individual Jewish soul, in an atmosphere of religious ecstacy.

Ironically, Hasidism today has come full circle and, if anything, has out-Rabbinated the Rabbis. Instead of a freer religious expression, Hasidism today is much more legalistic and punctilious about observing the full letter of the law to the extreme. The Mitnagdim of yesterday, were they alive today, would not recognize that the movement they had opposed has by now adopted virtually all the core observances and trimmings that they had originally protested against.

Another movement which established itself against the Rabbinic hierarchy was that of the Karaites. The Karaites, who sprouted forth in the 8th century, claimed that the Rabbis had misinterpreted the Bible, such that the original intentions of the Bible were lost in the mass of legislation that the Rabbis has piled upon the Biblical words. They, somewhat like the Reformers of today but with a totally different base, argued that all Jews had a right to explain the Bible according to their own views, and were not obliged to follow the official explanations that were offered by any of the sages. In effect, authority was to be vested in each individual.

The Karaites, to be sure, did not reject Mosaic legislation, as did the original Reformers. Instead, they argued for a return to the original Mosaic legislation unencumbered by Rabbinic exegesis. In so doing, the Karaites actually created a more stringent legalism. For example, the Bible asserts that one should not leave one's abode on the seventh day, the Shabbat. The Rabbinic explanation of this verse placed certain guidelines around leaving the city limits on the Shabbat, city limits being their understanding of what is meant by "abode." The Karaites insisted that this passage was an imperative to sit still at home on the seventh day.

With regard to the Biblical prohibition against burning a fire on the Shabbat, the Rabbinic explication of this verse allowed for making use of fire on the Shabbat if it had been kindled before the Shabbat and continued to burn unimpeded through the Shabbat itself. The Karaites, however, insisted that this Biblical commandment meant that no fire could burn in the home on the Shabbat. Thus, the Karaites sat in their places on Shabbat, had no heat, and ate cold food.

In a stunning paradox, the Karaites, who accused the Rabbis of distorting the Bible through their legalistic interpretations, actually created more severe burdens for their followers. It turned out that Rabbinic explication was much more livable. Also, the Karaites, whilst disclaiming the Rabbinic interpretations and the traditions emanating from these interpretations, nevertheless, by virtue of their own literal approach to the Bible, created traditions of their own, and not necessarily improvements upon the Rabbinic theme.

Additionally, and this has some relevance for the Reform movement of today, the Karaites, in insisting on allowing each individual to be the authority for his or her self, opened up a chaotic, subjective, self-serving approach which did not take into account the fact that the general public was really not so well informed about the intricacies of the Bible that they could make enlightened decisions. What was built up in the public mind as enlightened free choice degenerated quite quickly into arbitrariness and rejectionism become normative. Rejection of religious precepts was hallowed as a religion in itself!

On balance, these two movements, the Hasidic and the Karaitic, which originally were protestations against the Rabbinic mainstream, did not seriously alter the flow of Jewish history. The Karaites, thanks largely to the efforts of such individuals as Saadia Gaon, who effectively destroyed their theological base, more or less disappeared from the scene and did not make a significant dent in Jewish thinking. The Hasidim, as has been pointed out, whilst originally protesting against Rabbinic excess, most notably their application to the study of the law and strict code of observance whilst being aloof from the people, eventually came full circle, and today are proud standard bearers for punctilious observance of the halakhah. Almost invariably, they take the most stringent choices in halakhic observance.

There is, however, one movement, earlier than the Hasidic and Karaitic interjections, which impacted quite heavily on Jewish history, and continues to do so. I refer, of course, to Christianity. It is mind-boggling for a modern day observer to fully comprehend that less than two-thousand years ago Christianity was nothing more than a very minor sect operating within the Judaic context. The earliest Christians were Jews with some additional beliefs tacked on to those of their fellow Jews.

Any demographer living at that period in history could not have predicted that the Christian sect would evolve into a fully autonomous religion, a religion which would eventually vastly outnumber the Jewish religion. Considering that today there are approximately fourteen million Jews in the world and about one billion Christians, it is staggering to think that in the period of the turn of the century, just before the conflict with Rome, there were approximately eight million Jews in the world and a handful of those were Christians!

What happened since is a matter of history which merits some cursory examination. The Jews in the pre-Christian era actually made quite a noticeable impact on their surroundings. They attracted many people from outside the Jewish faith who had nothing but admiration for the high moral standards which were operative amongst Jews, and the sense of charity and philanthropy that was basic to Jewish life. Even such observances as the Shabbat, the seventh day, as a day of rest, with its celebration of the family and concentration on prayer and study, were also admired.

However, these outsiders had a problem. Much as they desired to glean from the superior standards amongst the Jews, it was difficult for them to convert outright to Judaism, since Judaism involved so many commandments and restrictions, do's and don'ts. Additionally, the demand for circumcision for males was not an easy pill for many an adult to swallow. Remember that this was before the age of anesthesia. There evolved, because of this, an unofficial group called "fearers of the Lord." These people, admiring Judaism, adopted some of the rituals and practices of Judaism as their own, but did not take the definitive step of conversion. They were half-Jews, even though from a technical, legalistic point of view there is no such entity as a half-Jew. These people frequented the synagogues, and grew up thinking that they were Jewish.

It should not be assumed that Judaism was universally admired. Many individuals, mostly pagan, saw in Judaism a challenge to their own religion, a challenge they chose to meet not by reemphasizing their own values, but by denigrating Jewish categories. Thus, the observance of the Shabbat became for some a symbol of Jewish laziness. The idea of belief in a God who had no shape or form was branded as superstition. And the fact that the Jews kept to themselves, observing their own celebrations whilst refusing to take part in pagan celebrations, showed that the Jews were a breed apart, and not a superior breed at that.

The blood libels that later became part of the Christian lexicon had their roots in the pagan opposition to Judaism. It was the pagans who fomented the passions of the populace against the Jews by charging that the Jews would occasionally capture a Greek, hide him in the Temple, and subsequently offer him up to God as a sacrifice. On balance, there were many more who denigrated Jews and Judaism than those who landed Jews and Judaism.

Originally, the Christians were a sect of Jews who, in addition to the basic Judaic beliefs and practices, added the belief that Jesus was the Messiah. After Jesus was crucified by the Romans, he was hidden away, and when the body was not found by his disciples a few days later, they despaired of his being the Messiah, but only for a fleeting period. They explained his disappearance as a unique phenomenon which presaged his coming again, or his second coming to redeem the world. Other than that, these Christians were Jews who observed all the regulations that were incumbent upon all Jews. An argument can be made for the proposition that on a percentage basis, they were more observant than the general Jewish population, amongst whom there were a high percentage of disaffected or assimilated Jews.

The key to Christianity's becoming a religion for the masses lies in the success of a dedicated missionary, Paul (Saul) of Tarsus, who originally was fascinated by Judaism but did not understand why Judaism was not accepted by the pagans, and indeed by many Jews. He started out with the intention of staunchly defending Jewish faith and practice. According to historical record, he was originally quite angry at the followers of Jesus for the belief that they professed. However, Paul was soon to change quite dramatically, after being inspired to split off Judaism into ideals and practices, and making the ideals of Judaism almost a self-contained system which would be attractive to the pagan world.

Paul, who travelled widely, tried firstly to impress Jews with his new theology, but they reacted vociferously against him when he would bring up the subject of Jesus' divinity, or when he would question the need for Jewish observance. Can ideals live without observance? Paul said yes, and the original Reformers also said yes. Judaism as we know it and as it has been transmitted through the generations has been a very delicate mix of ideals and practices, with the practices manifesting, in actual experience, the ethos of more theoretical ideals. The more Jews protested and rejected Paul, the more Paul went in an equal and opposite direction, protesting against Judaism and rejecting Jews. Paul received a the more theoretical ideals. The more Jews protested and rejected group which admired Judaism but felt uncomfortable with the stringent code of observance that was basic to Judaism.

It is not too difficult to project what must have happened to Paul as he was rejected by the Jews and accepted by the "fearers of the Lord." Pushed by the understandable rejection of the Jewish community for his aberrant theology, he probably went to an extreme in emphasizing the Jesus model, holding this up as the conduit to salvation. What evolved from this was a belief amongst the pagan element within the Christian sect that belief in Jesus was the necessary and sufficient condition to guarantee salvation. This was a very easy religion, and it catered almost magically to all those who had admired Judaism but felt it much too complex to be adopted as a lifestyle.

After the destruction of the Temple, in the year 70 of the common era, the Jews who professed belief in Jesus were at a distinct advantage. They had never acknowledged the primacy of the Temple, even identifying it as the seat of Jewish establishment which they rebelled against. When the Temple was destroyed, they could point to its destruction as an event which was consistent with their own beliefs, and could claim that this indicated God had abandoned the Jewish people. The new true Jews were the ones who believed in Jesus and forgot the Temple.

The destruction of the Temple was very significant, in that from that time on, the number of converts to Christianity was proportionately greater than the number of converts to Judaism. It did not take long for the Christian sect of Judaism to have a greater representation of non-Jews than Jews, even though this sect still was looked upon as a branch of Judaism.

Originally, believers in Jesus could be divided into two categories; those who saw themselves as Jews whilst still believing in Jesus, and those who believed in Jesus but had nothing to do with the Jews. Following the destruction of the Temple, as has been pointed out, the second group became the more weighty proportion of the Jesus cult. And these individuals, being in the main non-Jews, brought with them to this cult a fundamental antagonism to the Jews and Judaism, an antagonism which was rooted in the pagan contempt for the Jewish people.

The second critical event in the developing divorce of Christianity from Judaism was the Bar Kokhba revolt during the years 132 to 135 of the common era, and which followed the destruction of the Temple by a little more than sixty years, According to historical record, the Jewish Christians had until then been frequenters of the synagogue and participants in Jewish life. However, in the Bar Kokhba revolt, it became obvious that the Jews were fighting the battle against Rome alone, with both the Jewish Christians and the Gentile Christians being non-sympathetic, if not antagonistic to the Jewish cause.

Since the Christians believed that Jesus was the Messiah, they would have been terribly embarrassed had the Bar Kokhba revolt succeeded, since the Jews of that time saw Bar Kokhba as the Messiah. Some were even driven to become active opponents of the Jews. The Jews of that time, understandably riled by the treachery of the Christians, forcibly and permanently excluded the

Christians from Jewish communal life. They even added a prayer to the daily Amidah – the Amida being the major component of the prayer service consisting of eighteen benedictions, in which they asked that the Christian nemesis be removed from the face of the earth. It is interesting to note that in this violent interaction between Jews and Christians, the Jews asked God to take care of the dirty work, whereas the Christians, perhaps to protect their God as a God of love, engaged in the dirty work on their own. The Bar Kokhba revolt, then was that period in history when the budding separation became a permanent divorce.

The period following the Bar Kokhba revolt and its aftermath, saw the actualization of the truism that nature knows of no greater hate than that of love which is scorned. Child was now turning against parent, and with a vehemence and passion that was to affect hundreds of millions of lives from that time on. The Christians began to claim that God had rejected the Jewish people, that the Jews were a despicable people who performed blood rights with the innocent plasma of Christian children, a charge that undoubtedly emananted from the old canard that was levelled against the Jews by the pagans, who were the ancestors of the Christians.

Most detrimental from a historical perspective for the Jewish people was the all too successful attempt by the Christians to blame the Jews for the death of Jesus. Each new addition to the Christian testaments gradually reduced Roman implication in the crucifixion and at the same time escalated Jewish culpability in the crucifixion. The Christians indulged in a self-serving manipulation of history which, at one and the same time, reduced friction between the Christians and Romans and vilified the Jews as guilty of deicide, and who were therefore damned and doomed. This was to establish a gut-layer of hate in the Christian psyche which exploded in such horrendous historical episodes as the inquisition, the crusades, and the pogroms, and also established a pattern of hatred which was to consume European culture and cause unspeakable horror, up to and including the holocaust.

The early Christians were much more adept at the game of proselytizing. The doctrine which they were offering to the public, namely an easy salvation based on a very primitive belief system, that is to say – belief in Jesus, was just what the masses were looking for. Christianity was especially attractive to the great majority who were poor and had nothing in this world. The promise of salvation, and all of the grandeur of a world to come, was thus a great psychological, if not theological relief for these oppressed pople.

In the year 313 of the common era, the Roman emperor Constantine issued the famous edict of tolerance, which granted full toleration for all religions and restitution of the wrongs done to the Christians. Constantine himself converted to Christianity, and his own religious affirmation and policy escalated Christianity into a prominence that heretofore it had not experienced.

Once Christianity became prominent, an officially recognized religion which worked hand in hand with governmental authority, it became power hungry and power drunk, and used all the weapons at its disposal to obliterate the Jew and Judaism from the face of the earth. This came in the form of crusades, pogroms and other forms of terror encouraging Christians to get rid of the Jews, who, they claimed, had already been rejected by God. The all consuming hate which burned passionately within many a Christian was to set the stage for the most horrific crime in the history of civilization, the murder of six million Jews by the Nazis in the Second World War. So much for history.

Whilst it is always nice to invoke the famous warning that those who do not learn the lessons of history are doomed to repeat it, it should be noted that there are many differences between the condition of Judaism at the beginning of the common era and Judaism today. Firstly, the fact that Judaism has already gone through such a massive cataclysm, the Judaism-Christianity rupture, is enough reason to hope, if not to firmly believe, that history will not repeat itself. Secondly, whatever reasons may have then argued for the creation of a livable Judaism devoid of ritualistic norms are not relevant anymore, since today such a religion theoretically already exists, in the form of Christianity. On the other hand, it may be argued that Christianity today is so far removed from any Jewish ethos that those who would seek a stripped off form of Judaism probably would not be satisfied with Christianity.

Thirdly, whilst events at the dawn of the common era evolved into a lamentable, tragic reality for the Jewish people, the birth of Christianity did not in and of itself involve massive defections from Jewish ranks. As a matter of fact, Christianity owes its existence to the overwhelming proportion of non-Jews who joined Christian ranks. The antagonism to Judaism, to Rabbinism, was there, but it came in the vituperative doses essentially from pagan sources, and not from Jewish roots. The worry today is that there will be massive defections from Jewish ranks, splitting off either into a new religion, or into religionlessness.

It should be borne in mind that when Christianity surfaced as a variant form of Judaism, its constituents included many whose religious feelings were more intense than the general Jewish population, and who were more removed from the world, happy and content just to wait for their Messiah to arrive. This picture does not fit the description of modern Reform or those to the left of Reform. Whilst these individuals are concerned about religious categories, nevertheless even the belief in God itself is not a universal within the Reform context, and certainly not amongst the 40% of the population that is to the left of Reform. And even though the overwhelming proportion of the American population believes in God, this belief, it would appear, is merely a lip service gesture. And for some, saying they believe in God means simply that they do not believe in man, in the human capacity to create an ideal society.

Today it is not religious intensity that threatens to cause a rupture, rather a greater inclination to be part of society at large and to assimilate into the mainstream. There is thus a radical difference between the contemporary disenchanted and the early Christians, who went precisely in the opposite direction, the direction of withdrawal from society.

There have been great defections from Jewish ranks over the course of the centuries. It is hard to estimate, but it probably is not off the mark to suggest that Judaism lost as many to its ranks from assimilation as it did from murder by the enemy. Having gone through so many traumatic experiences in its history, it would be foolhardy for anyone to suggest that the separation of Reform and those to the left of Reform from the Jewish mainstream would spell the end of the Jewish people. Jewish resilience has been proven so many times that any predictions of demise must be treated with deserved skepticism.

It is not a question of whether Judaism will survive that is of concern. What is of concern is *how* Judaism will survive. Are the interests of Judaism, in terms of its own self and in terms of its relationship with and impact on the world, served by a defection of possibly half of its North American population? Does this type of cleavage not indicate a basic deficiency within Judaism itself, that after the holocaust and with the State of Israel, Judaism cannot sustain itself, it cannot maintain its sense of unity, and is crumbling apart, not able to keep the family together?

Since Reform is not a new phenomenon, and has been part of American Judaism for as long as Judaism has been a vibrant presence in North America, why should there be cause for alarm? The reason for being alarmist is that at this point in time, the North American reality is heading for disaster as far as the Jewish community is concerned. Never before in Jewish history have there been so many divorces and never before in Jewish history have there been so many conversions.

Twentieth century North America is the most democratic society that Jews have ever lived in. It is the most open, most liberal, most free flowing, and the most accepting, in spite of the problems of anti-semitism rearing its head here and there. Jews can occupy any position, Jews can travel in almost all social circles, Jews can mix with any segment of the population, and thus the prospects for increased assimilation are only more likely in the future. And this assimilation will come in megadoses from within Reform ranks and those to the left of Reform.

Additionally, the divorce rate in North America has already reached epidemic proportions, and most predictions are that it will get much worse before it gets better. If one out of every two marriages ends in divorce, as are the predictions right now, and if,

90

as far as can be estimated, the Jewish divorce rate will be just slightly behind the North American average, it stands to reason that divorce within Judaism will become a major problem. Already in New York City, by the end of the 1970's, it was estimated that close to forty thousand Jewish families were headed by a single parent.

Also, although there are no hard and fast statistics on this, the impression is that though there are quite a few divorces in Orthodox and Conservative ranks, they are not nearly as many as in Reform. This may be because of social pressures in Orthodoxy, which still does not look that favorably upon divorce. Whatever the case, Reform is slowly moving towards the situation when a large percentage of its clientele will either be non-Jewish, or, by virtue of a previous civil divorce following a Jewish marriage, will be plagued with problems of legitimacy. Included in this mix are previous members of Orthodox or Conservative congregations who, after a marital split, had trouble obtaining a religious divorce, and opted for Reform since the Orthodox and Conservative Rabbis were unwilling to sanction the second marriage, and only the Reform Rabbi was willing to officiate at the second marriage without a get. These types, not insignificant in number, are the most vexing when the matter of legitimacy is in question, since there is little ground for invalidating the first marriage.

This adds up to a problem of herculean proportions, of a social structure in which one segment of the Jewish population, namely the Orthodox and many of the Conservative, will be unwilling and unable to marry anyone from within Reform or to the left of Reform; unless, of course, the entire Jewish community bands together and intervenes to save itself.

In terms of the theological breakdown, how can the dark-side scenario evolve? To begin with, Reform today shares, although possibly to a lesser degree, an antagonism towards Rabbinism, towards the imposition of norms on the collective Jewish community via Rabbinic interpretation of Mosaic legislation. On the other hand, Reform today still espouses belief in the monotheistic ethos, even though it wrestles with the concept of God.

Christianity finally evolved on its own because of the influx into its ranks from the non-Jewish community. Reform too is in danger of having such a circumstance befall it, and this will especially be the case if the concept of patrilineal Judaism becomes its norm. Already today Reform is much more aggressive than the Conservative or Orthodox movements concerning conversion, and the type of conversion that is countenanced in Reform allows for entry into the Reform Jewish community of people who are slightly reminiscent of the "fearers of God" sect of yesteryear.

At the time of the Roman occupation of Israel, before the destruction of the Temple, no one could see Christianity evolving into a major religion, or even into an autonomous religion. It may have seemed more of a possibility following the destruction, but even then would have been considered an absurd prophecy. After the Bar Kokhba rebellion, it appeared to be more of a possibility, but even then the full magnitude of the situation could not have been predicted.

With the wisdom of hindsight, and realizing that the pundits then were totally baffled, it behooves the present generation of Jewish leadership to seriously contemplate the past miscalculations, to err on the side of caution so as to ensure that such miscalculations do not recur.

Today there are places where Reform congregations alternate services with a local church, with the church joining the Reform Temple on one weekend, and the Reform Temple joining the church on the other. There have been some Reform thinkers who have suggested Jews begin to acknowledge Jesus, not as a God, but at least as a prophet! With the growing sociological distance and the barriers that are being raised separating the Orthodox from the Reform, is it out of bounds to suggest that many who are presently identified as Jews could possibly swing over to a form of Judaism that is stripped of ritualistic imperative, somewhat like the Christians of old?

Is it outlandish to contemplate that a Hebrew Christian movement, a modern day counterpart to the Christian movement at the dawn of the common era, is a distinct possibility; and this, only as a buffer to total withdrawal from the Jewish community either by choice or by force of circumstance, the circumstance being the Orthodox rejection of the Reform community as non-Jewish, non-legitimate? There are today so many new cults, some of which will one day become institutionalized religions. Reform has suffered from disproportionately high numbers of defections to the cults. Who is to say that the disaffected Reform will not evolve into a cult-like group, as a first step towards establishing a new religious alternative? To say that it cannot happen is to defy history. To apply the statement, "never again," to this possibility, is to at least be alert to the dangers that will confront the Jewish community before too long if no preventive action is taken.

CHAPTER 12
DO NUMBERS MATTER?

The major thesis of this presentation has evolved around the potential defection and loss from Jewish ranks of possibly half of the present North American Jewish population. If this should occur, then the present approximately six million Jews of North America would be reduced in number to three million or thereabouts. Three million is not a lot, but it is also not a negligible amount. There have been times in the history of the Jewish people when the number of Jews was much less.

In the era before the Maccabean revolt, some estimates have it that there remained only a handful of Jews who were steadfast in their commitment to Judaism. Still, Judaism survived that very perilous situation, one which came too close to spelling the end of the Jewish people. Jewish history has been a history of narrow escapes from disappearance. That being the case, why should we worry about the possibility of the North American Jewish population going down from six million to three million?

Some demographers have made the assessment that, given the present rate of assimilation in Jewish ranks, and coupled with the present fertility rate, the Jewish population is likely to anyway diminish to approximately three million by the tercentenary of the United States, in 2076. Those demographers did not contemplate the critical condition facing the North American Jewish community, a situation spelled out in this volume, and threatening to explode long before the tercentenary.

If one combines the assimilation and fertility factors with the tragedy of separation, the Jewish population of North America in another hundred years or so could be even less than three million. With all this, no one can predict, based on any historical precedent, that this spells the end of the Jews. If the Jews could survive with a handful, they could certainly survive with a few million.

The question, again, is not whether they can survive with two or three million, but how they will survive? Will they survive as a vibrant faith community, or will they be like a maimed horse, running about the track but barely making it to the finish line? If the theological volcano erupts, and the right and left wings of the Jewish corpus split asunder into separate and distinct religions, Judaism will not only be affected numerically, but also theologically.

The Judaism of the right, which would be seen as the natural extension of Talmudic Judaism, would undoubtedly be a very militant religion, if present trends are any indication. This group, which is presently proliferating at the highest rate, and which can claim a foothold on the Judaism of the future, is not that actively involved in communal affairs, has not created a sphere of influence in the North American community, and is predominantly isolationist. That type of Judaism, in a free democratic society, cuts itself off from one of the major ideals of Judaism; specifically, the spreading of Jewish ideals to the world at large.

Sharing Judaism with the world is not conceived as a missionizing imperative. Judaism has no responsibility to go out and urge individuals to change their faith. Judaism is not a racist religion by any stretch. It has never claimed to possess the only keys to paradise. Righteousness is the universal Esperanto for gaining a foothold on eternality. Those who want can become Jewish, no matter what their color or ethnic origin. Judaism is a set of values, no more and no less. It is available to anyone, but imposed on no one outside Judaic ranks. Jews have no desire to make the world Jewish, but they do desire, or at least should desire to make the world good, if not better.

Thus Judaism from the very outset has not been shy about espousing humanistic ideals and a higher code of morals and ethics that should be adopted by the world at large. But Judaism cannot expect the world at large to adopt these values, if these selfsame values are not lived out by Jews, and are instead rejected. Thus, it is extremely vital that whatever Jewish community exists in any free society be unabashedly, even zealously affirmative of Jewish values and willing to share of itself, to impart to the world the beauty of Judaism. Failing that, Judaism would surely survive, but it would not be the classical Judaism that was envisaged by the prophets of yesteryear to be a light unto the nations of the world. Instead, it would be a crippled version of the dynamic ideal.

Numbers, then, do matter in this instance, even though what is being projected here is just one person's speculation. But numbers matter for other reasons too. It is well known that any group, in order to maintain a sense of vibrancy, needs to maintain what is referred to as a critical mass, a solid population base which is able, through the sheer force of numbers, to create and maintain vibrant institutions which serve as source and resource to inspire communal growth, and guarantee the continuity of that community.

The Jewish community being cut down from six million to three million would impact heavily on the critical mass, and would certainly cut down on the number of institutions, be they synagogues, schools, community centers, social service agencies, etc., that are geared to help the greater Jewish community. With these resources falling victim to the population attrition, the impact will be heavily felt on those who have been fotunate enough to survive the cataclysm. The quality of Jewish life will be severely affected, and adversely so, by such a precipitous drop in the number of Jews.

But there is more to the issue than the affect of such a massive drop in the Jewish population on Jewish institutional life. The affect of such a drop on the collective Jewish psyche could be nothing less than disastrous. How will Jews be able to look themselves in the mirror, knowing that so many of their brethren have left the fold, and they could have done something about it, indeed should have done something about it, but did not? Is there any greater crime that they could have committed against the Jewish community than such gross neglect? The answer is no, they would know that the answer is no, and therefore they would feel a deserved sense of shame for having allowed this to happen.

Undoubtedly, once it has happened, the surviving Jewish community will band together and try to devise strategies for solidifying the remnant, for ensuring that the tragedy they have experienced never happens again, and perhaps even increasing their own ranks through a renewed committment to greater families. But all this is mere window-dressing that would not effectively cover up the reality that three million lost souls, many of whom could have been saved from going over the theological precipice, were left to their own devices, with no effective, coherent communal effort to forestall this traumatic event.

Judaism today is still in the process of analyzing what happened during the holocaust. We have just begun to properly lament the loss of six million Jews, the tragedy of the partially successful attempt to eliminate Jews and Judaism from the face of the earth. Why did it happen? Why did the world allow it to happen? How could such hate erupt from the human soul and behave, with premeditation, in such a violently despicable manner? Did the Jews resist or did they allow it to happen? Did the Jews, in countries where free expression was allowed, effectively mount protestations to forestall further tragedy, or were they asleep at the switch? What have been the effects of the holocaust on the survivors, the children of the survivors, the children of the children of survivors, etc? The holocaust is perhaps the primary subject occupying Jewish thinkers today. And this has filtered down to the grass roots level. There is nary a city of significant Jewish population that does not have some visible memorial to the six million.

However, if we allow three million more Jews to slip out of the Jewish grasp, we will have many questions to answer, and the answers may not be adequate. The major question will be, how can we at one and the same time lament the loss of six million Jews, and yet allow for the present loss of three million more Jews through lack of massive effort by the community to forestall such a tragedy? Is there any worse commentary on the holocaust than to allow for even more Jewish losses in our own time, in an era which is so sensitive to the holocaust, and is just beginning to wrestle with post-holocaust trauma in an effective manner? Is there any greater contradiction than to be concerned about yesterday's loss whilst at the same time being blind to tomorrow's tragedy? Allowing the cataclysm to unfold will have branded as partially fraudulent all our concern about making recompense for the past, or trying to somehow or other make sense out of the present in the light of the past. If this is done at the expense of the future, then it is not only an exercise in futility, it is verily a theological disgrace.

Then there is the matter of Russian Jewry. The North American Jewish community, indeed Jewish communities all over the world that are allowed free expression, have raised their voices in unison against the oppressive policies of the Soviet government towards its three million or more Jews. We have collectively and individually demanded, through our own protestations, and through our representations to local representatives and to the governments of the countries in which we reside, that pressure be brought to bear on the Soviet Union to allow Jews free expression of their religion in Soviet Russia, and that those individuals who so desire be granted their legitimate right to leave the Soviet Union to live freely as Jews in the land of Israel.

The efforts of the collective Jewish community have had an inspiring effect on the Jews of Russia, who have been heartened and re-invigorated by the knowledge that their brethren outside the Soviet Union are fighting their fight and espousing their cause. But what would be the reaction of the Jews of Russia if they learn that three million Jews, symbolizing the same number as the Jews of the Soviet Union, have left Jewish ranks, and disappeared into religionlessness, or into a divergent religion? What effect will this have on the Jews of Russia, who have risked their lives and their well-being in order to maintain their Jewishness, or in order to be granted the right to leave the Soviet Union to live as Jews in Israel?

What effect will this have on the Jewish communities around the world who are struggling for the establishment of religious freedom in Russia? How will they answer those who say that it is ridiculous to ask for this free expression, when, in places where the Jews do have free expression, that free expression becomes "good-by Jews, good riddance Judaism?" If the Jewish sojourn in the free world is doomed to failure, as proven by this radical and traumatic rupture, what is there to fight for? It is an exercise which is doomed to failure even in the best of conditions, so that the Jews might as well give up the ghost and forget the fight.

We come now to the final point in tackling the question of do numbers matter? It is true that throughout the ages Judaism has struggled, and pulled itself up from the brink of extinction on numerous occasions. But every time Judaism brought itself back from the brink of extinction, and was able to thrive even in hostile environments, Jews could point to the fact that their coming perilously close to extinction was through no fault of their own, but through an oppressive despot or a lynch mob population which did not allow them to live. Only through some miraculous deliverance were they able to escape, or at least were granted the "privilege" of remaining, although with limited rights and with limited freedoms.

In the 20th century, the Jews have had an opportunity unprecedented in their history. This is the opportunity to live as equals, true equals with society at large in an enlightened democracy, such as the United States or Canada. Surely there should be no problem now with Jewish survival. Surely there should be no problem with Jewish vibrancy. Surely there should be no problem with Judaism not only maintaining itself, but flourishing, proliferating, and making a definite impact on society.

But what happens? Instead of Judaism being vibrant, instead of Judaism flourishing, it does to itself what others have done to it over the course of the generations. Instead of unifying, instead of developing a coherent community which in spite of differences works together for common causes, Judaism splits apart, and a significant number falls by the theological wayside and is totally lost to Jewish ranks.

What right does Judaism have to lament the failures of the past, the fact that its population was periodically decimated and Judaism itself denied its proper place in the history of the world and in the development of human ideals? Are we resorting to the absurd charge that by others murdering us, they are taking away our right to commit suicide? Judaism, by disintegrating in such massive numbers, will have denied its ancestry, will have transmuted the triumphs of yesterday's martyrs into present and future tragedy, and will have failed miserably in the most ideal laboratory in which Judaism could ever function.

We could survive in North America with only three million committed Jews. Whether we could survive a precipitous drop from six million to three million, and the theological-sociological-psychological fallout from such an explosion, is another matter. Can Judaism really claim to be a light unto the nations when it is a blight unto itself?

SECTION 4
PROJECTIONS

CHAPTER 13
FUTURE REFORM

The question of where Reform is heading is extremely vital for the future of the North American Jewish community, because, when the statistics are distilled, it turns out that the Reform constituency is significantly larger than the constituency of the Conservative and the Orthodox. The Orthodox constituency is comprised of those who are committed to Orthodox belief, and ideally, also to Orthodox practice. The Conservative constituency is made up of those who are committed to the Conservative world view, combining adherence to, or connection with tradition, with some semblance and sprinkling of modernity. The doses of modernity and traditionalism vary from house to house and from congregation to congregation.

The Reform constituency, however, is significantly larger because it may include not only the Reform Jews themselves, but also the approximately 40% who are non-affiliated Jews, far away from any significant Jewish commitment, and who would probably turn to the Reform option if religion ever became a matter of import. If a Rabbi would be necessary to officiate at an event, be it subsequent to birth, for marriage, a funeral, or whatever, the overwhelming majority of these individuals would lean towards calling a Reform Rabbi.

Potentially then, although not actually, Reform has access to a greater percentage of the North American Jewish population. However, as is the case with the Conservative and the Orthodox, where the Reform Rabbinate is at is not where the Reform constituency is at. Orthodox, Conservative, and Reform Judaism can boast of dedicated followers who sometimes embarrass the leadership with their zeal. However, in the main, the religious commitment and dedication of the respective Rabbis is much more intense, usually much better informed, and therefore of a much more profound quality than that of the congregants.

Many an Orthodox Rabbi ministers to a congregation which is perhaps twenty or twenty-five percent Orthodox, with the rest, for all intents and purposes, being either Conservative or Reform in their practice. The Conservative Rabbi likely has a higher percentage that would somehow or other fit into the broad spectrum of Conservative Judaism, with a significant percentage probably leaning towards Reform. The Reform congregation likely is made up of a small percentage who are dedicated to living out Reform ideology to the full, with the rest just barely identifying in order not to fall totally by the wayside, but showing little desire to take an extra step in the theological dimension.

It is therefore difficult to assess the future of the Reform movement based solely on where the Rabbis in Reform are at. The

Rabbis in Reform may be coming closer and closer to Conservative Judaism, not merely for political expediency as is the case in Israel, but also because the attitude towards tradition is changing in Reform circles. However, this does not necessarily mean that the lay community in Reform will follow the example and the leadership that is shown by its Rabbis. Still, the examination of where the Reform Rabbinical leadership is at will provide some important insights which may help in making an educated guess about where Reform Judaism will be a few decades from now.

Perhaps the best indication of where Reform Judaism is at, or at least where the hierarchy of Reform Judaism is at, may be gleaned from a study of the Centenary Perspective, the 1976 document giving an indication of the Reform ideology concerning such matters as God, the Jewish people, religious practice, and the State of Israel. In the background of the Pittsburgh Platform of 1875 and the Columbus Platform of 1937, the Centenary Perspective makes for fascinating reading, and for interesting insights into the direction toward which the Reform leadership is heading.

In the Pittsburgh Platform, Reform asserted that it no longer considers the Jewish people a nation, but only a religious community, and does not expect a return to Palestine or the restoration of any laws concerning the Jewish State. The 1937 Columbus Platform made an about-face, calling what was then referred to as Palestine as the land that was hallowed by memories and hopes, and stating that Reform affirms the obligation of all Jews to aid in the building of Palestine as the Jewish homeland. This homeland is to serve not only as a refuge for those who live in oppressed countries; it is also to become a spiritual and cultural center for the global Jewish community.

The Centenary Perspective went even further, affirming a deep and abiding connection with the State of Israel, and insisting that Reform has a stake and a responsibility in building the State of Israel. And amazingly, the Centenary Perspective actually encourages Aliyah (*going up* to Israel) "for those who wish to find maximum personal fulfillment in the cause of Zion." Only someone who has thoroughly studied the birth of Reform can fully appreciate the significance of this statement. For Reform to encourage Aliyah is literally to go full circle from its original antipathy to the concept of a Jewish State.

Of course one can detect in this encouraging of Aliyah that which is indigenous to Reform; specifically, the way in which Aliyah is encouraged. It is not imposed, but rather it is proposed as an option for those who find fulfillment, personal fulfillment in the Zionist cause. This means that going to Israel, in the Reform context, is done as a means for personal fulfillment, or at least that is the basis for the decision. It is not seen as an obligation but rather as an option that can be exercised by those who would find personal usefulness in exercising this option.

This is typical of the approach that Reform takes to the fulfillment of any mitzvah. That approach is geared to preserving the notion of individual choice, the right and the privilege, even the responsibility of every Reform Jew to make choices concerning what elements of the Jewish religious tradition he or she wants to adopt and espouse. The Reform attitude, as it has evolved in the Centenary Perspective, encourages the Jew to choose *from the tradition*. There is no obligation to choose the tradition itself, but rather to choose that which is individually attractive from the tradition.

Reform has come to the point where it feels that it must confront the tradition. It is acknowledged that Reform actually did not start Judaism, and Reform Jews should seriously contemplate whether the religious practices of previous generations should not in fact be the Reform mode. Whether or not each individual Reform Jew decides to make the past traditional lifestyle the contemporary way of Jewish expression is a personal decision, but a decision that needs to be made on the basis of commitment and, of course, knowledge about the tradition. To make a decision as to how to be a Jew without knowing anything about Judaism is, in the perspective of the Centenary, foolhardy.

Reform is actually going through a crisis with regard to the issue of prescription of norms; what is, in the Jewish parlance, the adoption of a code of rules, or a Reform halakhah. There are Reform Jews who, seeking direction about what and how to actualize, would appreciate guidelines and a reasonably definitive code. On the other hand, there are those who insist that the Reform notion of autonomy cannot be compromised.

The Centenary Perspective reached some form of compromise solution, stating that the actual choice as to what to observe need not be mandated, but there are certain areas of life, even Jewish life, in which each Jew should be doing something, or at least thinking about doing something before deciding to do nothing! Thus, in the areas of study, prayer, family life, Shabbat, holy days, and other observances, it was decided that there is a responsibility for each Jew to do something about Jewish religious categories. What they do in these areas remains a personal decision, but something should be done. This is a compromise which somehow or other maintians the notion of freedom but at the same time introduces the element of tradition, although not making of the traditions a required form of behavior.

The perspective on this change, looking at it from a telescopic view of Reform history, is as astounding a turnabout as is the Reform change with regard to a Jewish State. The original Pittsburgh Platform maintained that all Mosaic and Rabbinic laws regulating diet or dealing with dress or priestly purity were, for all intents and purposes, archaic practices that did not relate to contemporary times. They did not in any way invest the Jew with a sense of holiness, and instead were an obstruction to spiritual elevation.

The Columbus Platform moved away from that position, and stressed that Judaism is not merely a way of life making moral and spiritual demands. Judaism also requires the preservation of the Shabbat and the festivals, as well as the retention and development of customs, ceremonies and practices which have inspirational value.

The Centenary Perspective went even further. It asserted that even though the founding fathers of Reform stressed the Jew's ethical, personal, and social responsibilities, yet the past century has taught Reform that the claims made upon the Jew do not end with the ethical obligations. Instead, they extend to other aspects of Jewish life, including a Jewish home with family devotion, study, private and public prayer, observance of some religious nature on a daily basis, the keeping of the Shabbat and the holy days, celebration of the major events of life, continued involvement with the synagogue and community, and all such activities which promote the possibilities of Jewish survival and enhance Jewish existence. It is within these areas of Jewish observance that Reform Jews are called upon to "confront the claims of Jewish tradition, however differently perceived, and to exercise their individual autonomy, choosing and creating on the basis of commitment and knowledge."

When one reads the three documents, the Pittsburgh Platform of 1875, the Columbus Platform of 1937, and the 1976 Centenary Perspective, it is quite obvious that Reform is coming closer and closer to tradition, if the frame of reference is the position espoused by Reform leadership. Israel and the kosher code, amongst other practices, were just about read out of Jewish tradition in 1875, but they have verily been resurrected, and now form a very significant component of Reform ideology.

Still, Reform has not swallowed the "obligation pill." This reflects the consensus amongst the Reform Rabbinic leadership, which is polarized on the issue of obligation, but agreeable to a frame of reference which allows for both the autonomy oriented and the halakhically oriented Reformists to feel comfortable.

To achieve this middle-ground position, the Centenary Perspective opens up tradition as a very viable option, but urges each and every Jew to make his or her own decision. In other words, even the Rabbi cannot impose traditions upon the congregation. Instead, the Rabbi can merely teach some of these traditions, make the congregation aware of these traditions, or at least those of the congregation who are concerned enough to learn, and then say to them – okay, now that you know what it is all about, it is up to you. It is a personal choice; you can either take it or leave it, or take part of it, or take most of it, or take none of it.

How long will Reform be able to hold to this position? It is reasonably certain that if this position is adopted and carried through seriously, Reform will establish itself as a permanent hodge-podge in which each and every individual will do as he or she pleases. To assume that every Reform Jew will make an enlightened decision based on thorough study of Jewish tradition is to be as naive as the Karaites were centuries ago. Most Jews today, unfortunately, have made their decision as to what they will observe based not on thorough study, but based on what is personally convenient. What is personally convenient usually evolves as a lifestyle that maintains some linkage with parental tradition, but is not nearly as intense or as demanding. How long will it take for Reform to bend to the pressure, and provide definitive guidelines which establish the bottom line common denominator for Reform Jewish practice; not only to satisfy those who seek direction, but to prevent Reform from disintegrating into arbitrariness?

Judging by the pattern that Reform is taking, and the increasing sensitivity of Reform to Jewish tradition, it would not be out of bounds to predict that before long Reform may evolve distinctive traditions of its own. Then too, it will have gone the way of the Karaites, starting off by rejecting Mosaic and Rabbinic legislation, but then turning around and creating legislation of their own. Needless to say, such a move by the Reform leadership will probably precipitate a crisis within Reform ranks. Those who reject the imposition of required disciplines will either leave the fold, or reject that plank. Reform, at that point in time, will have essentially created its own Orthodoxy!

There is an irony to the present Reform position, which should not be lost on the Reform leadership. Basically, Reform, in insisting on free choice, is not really running contrary to Biblical tradition. After all, it was in the Bible itself that the original Israelites, and thus Jews in every generation, were asked to make a choice between life and the good, and death and the bad. The exhortation,spelled out in the Bible, asks all individuals to "choose life." But it is the type of choice which each individual is urged to make.

The demand for guidelines, the demand for discipline and tradition, speaks to the fundamental human desire to transcend present conditions. Perhaps it is grounded in the belief that religion should take the individual beyond where the individual would go alone. Religion pulls the individual further than the individual would ever push his or her own self. The Reform accent on individual choice is too heavily oriented towards a push type of religion, and is missing the transcendent perspective. The yearning for direction is essentially a yearning for a transcendental pull which will uplift individuals to a point of elevation that could not be reached by subjective self-expression.

When the Bible asks the Jew to choose, it does not ask the Jew to pick and choose, it asks the Jew to choose. The choice that the Bible speaks about is a transcendent choice, or a commitment to adopt the entire package, not just to pick out bits and pieces that are personally gratifying and easy to actualize. It is a choice which uplifts, because it is a choice which involves unconditional commitment to the whole.

The irony of the present Reform position is that if it is carried through to the letter, it can only work if the entire smorgasbord of Jewish options is mapped out before Reform congregants. How else can Reform Jews choose from the tradition, and have a true and broad choice, unless they are presented with the full range of choices. Seeing the entire platter of Jewish observances, it is then up to each and every Reform Jew to decide his or her own personal menu. But if the smorgasbord is a complete one, it is not outside the realm of possibility that some Reform Jews may take the entire menu; or, in simple terms, they will take the Orthodox option.

This means that Reform, in the accommodating stance that it takes to tradition, opens up the possibility that its clientele may, in its choice of observance, range anywhere from complete Orthoxy to the negation of all. But this type of evolution did not really need Reform. Jews in each generation, and certainly in the 20th century, have that full range of possibilities without need for a Reform movement. Based on the availability of all these options, the question remains; what is Reform achieving that could not be achieved just by letting individuals choose whatever traditions they want to observe, a choice that existed before, during, and after Reform intervention on the Jewish scene?

Many Reform Jews take pride in the fact that they light the candles for Shabbat on Friday night. They assert that by so doing, they identify with the Jewish heritage. It is for them a very meaningful experience.

The question that may be posed to such individuals is; by what dynamics does the fact of lighting candles form a linkage with Jewish tradition? There are tribes in Afghanistan that do exactly the same thing on Friday night, which has led some observers to claim that they may be from the ten lost tribes. However, for these tribes the lighting of the candles is a practice, but certainly not one which links them with the Jewish community.

In fact lighting of candles merely initiates a combustion process. What gives it its Jewish imprimatur? The answer is a simple one. Jews from the earliest times brightened their homes on Friday night as ordained by the Rabbis. It is a fulfillment of the obligation to have a Shabbat which glorifies God, which glorifies the human being, and which glorifies time. The constant repetition, the dedication to this practice, as indeed the dedication to other pracices, is what has made the lighting of candles on Friday night for the Shabbat an inspiring traditon, one amongst many practices which links with the Jewish past and forges the Jewish future.

But it would be ludicrous for anyone to claim that this identity exercise has sprung spontaneously from nowhere. Thus, even when engaging in optional traditions, Reform Judaism is sinking its roots all the way back to that which effectively was Orthodox religious expression. Reform leadership is increasingly recognizing the role of tradition, and the fact that the options for tradition, which relate back to the Jewish past, are not as archaic for Reform now as they were in the days of the Pittsburgh Platform and prior to that.

Reform leadership cannot help but realize that on balance, the Reform experiment is heading towards catastrophe. Surely there are those in Reform who are motivated by a strong dose of sincerity, and are authentically in quest of spiritual betterment. But there are too many others for whom Reform is just an excuse for unconditional rejection of Judaism with just a token form of identification. The exceedingly high rate of assimilation in Reform, coupled with the low birth rate, does not make for an optimistic picture of future Reform.

It should not be surprising that this is the case, since Reform is letting its clientele make all the decisions. But unfortunately, the decisions that they are making too often abuse the license that has been given in this most serious matter, the affirmation of Jewishness. So what that the Reform population need not feel guilty about their choice, since that choice is legitimized by the Rabbinic leadership. Still, the results of that choice spell catastrophe for the Reform movement, and hence for a very large segment of the North American Jewish population. Today, we are ever so cautious about laying a guilt trip on people. But there is a flip side to the elimination of guilt. As soon as guilt is removed from human endeavor, the will to change goes with it. By feeling guilty, the desire to remove the guilt through improved behavior, a penance of sorts, is evoked. In the Reform context, lacking the will to change serves to institutionalize stultification and locks Reform into a present with no future, because there is no past, no immutable tradition.

Reform undoubtedly will be faced with a complicated and burdensome choice a few decades down the road. That choice will be concerning where it should lead its people; either into the religious matrix which will probably by then be primarily Orthodox, or into an autonomous existence free from involvement with the Orthodox. A large part of that decision will depend on how Reform reacts in the next number of years to the challenge posed by the divorce and conversion avalanche threatening to permanently separate the Orthodox and Reform communities.

The right decision by Reform will be a salvational exercise for a large segment of the 60% of the population with which Reform has most direct contact. Undoubtedly, there will be attrition, attrition that even Reform cannot forestall, but the massive, catastrophic losses that could occur would be avoided if Reform makes the right moves in the next little while. Ironically, via rapprochement with the Orthodox, Reform very likely may at the same time preserve its own self.

CHAPTER 14
FUTURE ORTHODOXY

What is true of Reform is true to a large extent of Orthodoxy. It should not be assumed that Orthodoxy is a monolith, a singular group gathered together under one banner, and espousing the same ideals. Basically, Orthodoxy shares in common a commitment to living out God's word through the Torah, as explicated in the Talmud, the commentaries, responsa literature, and legal codes which followed.

But there are many variations upon the theme, and the life-styles of different groupings that come under the heading of Orthodox vary greatly. Under the rubric of Orthodox one would be obliged to include the Hasidic groups, including Lubavitch, Satmar, and the like, as well as the Orthodoxy of the yeshiva stripe, Young Israel type Orthodoxy, modern Orthodoxy, and other variant forms.

There is at the same time much ferment within Orthodoxy, intellectual ferment concerning certain issues and attitudes that are espoused by the Orthodox. Perhaps the most ubiquitous source of ferment surrounds the attitude to the State of Israel. Here the Neturei Karta (watchers of the city), a movement of Satmar ideoogy which is virulently anti-Zionist, has caused no end of embarrassment to other Orthodox groups, precisely because it is identified as a very militantly Orthodox and at the same time militantly anti-Zionist group.

Many pro-Israel groups among the Orthodox take great pains to dissociate themselves from having anything to do with the Satmar stance concerning Zionism. Some have even suggested that Satmar institutions, such as those pertaining to kashruth, should be boycotted in order to show detachment in a radical fashion from Satmar ideology.

There is another not so obvious area of ferment within Orthodoxy, and the issue has not yet been spelled out in clear-cut terms, yet, but that is only around the corner. It deals with two trends within Orthodoxy, the one trend towards introspection, or more precisely, introversion on a communal scale, the other trending towards extraversion, and concern for the greater Jewish community, including the Conservative and the Reform.

The more rightish elements in Orthodoxy, whilst concerned about the future of the Jewish community and lamenting the high rate of assimilation as well as the declining birth rate, nevertheless do not reach out into the community per se, and have very little contact with the non-Orthodox. If there is any cross fertilization, it comes simply because people from non-Orthodox backgrounds venture into the Orthodox experience and are exposed to the Orthodox environment. The return of many, what has been referred to as the Baal Tshuva movement, is perhaps the primary manifestation of this phenomenon. But this movement toward Orthodoxy is on Orthodoxy's terms. Otherwise, Orthodoxy takes a dim view of any Orthodox involvement, on an official level, with the non-Orthodox community.

But it does not end there. Usually, those who espouse non-involvement with the non-Orthodox community on an official level have very little to do with the non-Orthodox even on an unofficial level. One may say that to a certain extent the non-Orthodox have been read out of the Jewish pale, although one hopes that this is not an irreversible judgment.

The other trend within Orthodoxy is towards the extraversion posture, evincing a manifest concern for the non-Orthodox, getting together with them on official and unofficial levels, and maintaining meaningful communication and cross fertilization of thoughts and ideas.

This trend within Orthodoxy has set out to achieve the very reverse. It has attempted to integrate the Conservative, the Reform and others into the matrix of concern for the Jewish future, and is making definitive strides towards meaningful intergroup co-operation. The more right wing element within Orthodoxy looks with suspicion upon the motives of these Orthodox moderates; the moderates themselves look upon the rightish elements within Orthodoxy as obscurantist at the very least.

What will the Orthodoxy of tomorrow look like? Realistically, the likelihood of a split within Orthodoxy cannot be ruled out of the realm of possibility. Already, there are indications that certain elements within Orthodoxy see the modern Orthodox as the greatest danger to Torah-true Judaism, and have as much as made public statements to this effect. What is today branded as modern Orthodoxy and therefore has at least some credibility in the eyes of the more zealous Orthodox, could become, in time, combined with continuing ferment and alienation, a movement which is read out of the Torah-true Judaism context. The end result of this polarization is that present day Modern Orthodoxy could somehow become branded as a neo-Conservative movement, because the hawkish Orthodox insist that it does not adhere to the principles which define Orthodoxy. If that should happen, it would further brand Orthodoxy as an isolationist group which has shut itself off from the greater community.

To those who say let them be, let them shut themselves off from the community, it should be noted that right-wing Orthodoxy is today the most vibrant religious group in the North American Jewish community. It has some of the most hyperactive institutions, including overflowing houses of prayer, houses of study, and higher institutions of learning. All this is in response to the demands that are placed upon the right-wing Orthodox due to an increasing birthrate, averaging between five and six per family, and also their constituents marrying at an early stage in life such that they are squeezing in more generations per century than the modern Orthodox, the Conservative, and the Reform. Politically, they can get out the vote, theologically they can exercise clout, and communally they can have a decided impact on the future of the North American Jewish community, for weal or for woe. Orthodoxy has too many much needed resources, reservoirs of tradition, which, if not fed into the larger community, will lead to spiritual emaciation.

Looking at the total picture, the potential is therefore a not so inviting prospect in the North American Jewish community. We have the prospect of Orthodoxy splitting down the middle, Reform splitting down the middle, and the Conservative movement forced, perhaps by virtue of its being caught in the middle, to move either more towards the left or more towards the right, but essentially not being a major player in the unfolding saga of North American Jewry. The saga that is unfolding is one of more rupture, more civil strife, less coherence, less unity; in a word, massive problems.

Unless those who are responsible for leading the community, the leadership hierarchy in all sectors, take the proverbial bull by the horns and say – enough is enough, the community is in peril and we must forget rationalizations, name-calling and petty banner-waving politics; failing that the Jewish community threatens to splinter off into sectarian groupings, and to the potential catastrophe that has been outlined in previous chapters.

Orthodox leadership has a responsibility to greater Israel, not merely to the Orthodox community. The rule that if one sees a fellow Jew in danger, one is obligated to do whatever one can to save that person's life, does not obligate us to ask whether that person is an Orthodox Jew, a Conservative Jew, or a Reform Jew. The person is Jewish and we have an obligation to act. Where the danger is not so clear cut, and is instead a danger of assimilation so that one's Jewish moorings are dislodged from their proper anchorage, we do not perceive the emergency or the halakhic urgency as clearly, but it is there. Those who are sensitive enough about halakhah to expound to the community what the halakhah says about Shabbat, kashruth, and other such items, must do the same concerning the question of saving not merely a remnant, but a major component of the Jewish fabric.

It is in a certain sense dangerous to suggest the following proposition, but within certain limitations, it can be argued in hindsight that rebellious actions that have been taken in reaction to a specific, established group are not void of some merit. It is the broad application of the truism that in most conflicts, the issue is not black and white. One side may be more correct than the other, depending on whom you ask, but rarely is one side totally in the right and the other completely wrong.

Without in any way trying to denigrate any individual or group of individuals, it is conceivable that the rejection of Rabbinism throughout the generations, whether it came at the turn of the century from the Christian sect, whether it came from the Karaites, whether it came from the Hasidim, or whether it came from the Reform, was in some measure due to a perception of the Judaism being espoused, a perception which did not click with the pre-conceived ideal.

Undoubtedly, there were many assimilationists who were looking for an excuse to Reform; undoubtedly there were many Karaites who were interested in causing trouble just for the sake of mischief, or for ego satisfaction. But the fact that the espoused rebelliousness and new approach met with some measure of positive communal response indicates that something was disturbing the community. Perhaps that something was not so significant, something which was submerged and possibly would have remained submerged. But perhaps it was a Judaism which was too severe, a Judaism which was too austere, a Judaism which projected itself as being too demanding.

We tend to take the attitude that these movements were dissident movements, historical aberrations, and that therefore, as aberrations, they should be dismissed as insignificant. But when it happens so often, and when these dissident movements can attract such significant followings, it is cavalier just to simply ignore. Perhaps there is something about the Orthodox lifestyle that is self-limiting, and that gives birth from generation to generation to anti-Orthodox feelings, which when they conglomerate in large doses, become an anti-Orthodox movement. An Orthodoxy which refuses to seriously contemplate this possibility is not honest with itself, and is not equal to its responsibility.

The corpus of Jewish law is essentially divided into two major categories; those laws or commandments (mitzvot) which deal with the relationship between the human being and God, and those commandments which deal with interpersonal relations. The prophets long ago railed against those who specialized in the ritual side of the commandments, but simultaneously showed great insensitivity to their fellow beings. The prophets saw this as a gross distortion of the essence of Judaism.

Throughout the generations there have been those who think that they are consistent with the message of the prophets in that they also emphasize the ethical. But the prophets never intended to emphasize the ethical at the expense of the ritual, but rather to emphasize that the ritual without the ethical is bankrupt; from God's point of view a distortion of the intent of the ritual. Judaism has had saints, many saints whose behavior in both the ritual and human spheres has been impeccable, but the feeling persists amongst many that scrupulous adherence to ritual law does not necessarily make for a better person.

Too often there are individuals who are so exacting and demanding with regard to ritualistic practices but are less than demanding and exacting in the sphere of human relations, where they land up being quite deficient. The impression which remains is that individuals who are very strict with Shabbat observance, or with adherence to kashruth regulations, feel that they have earned some sort of divine right to be above ethical prescription. They can do what they please in the human sphere since they have already earned their spurs with God by virtue of their intensive ritualistic commitment.

If the ritual side of observerance does not feed positively into the ethical sphere, then one can assuredly state that there is something fundamentally wrong, at the core, with the schizoid-like ritualistic commitment. The ritual, as God's word, needs to be observed for no other reason than because it is God's word. But if it is observed because it is God's word, then anything which is God's word must be observed with equal intensity of application.

An individual who chooses to commit the self to keeping the Shabbat, to adhering to the kosher code, but at the same time chooses to be less than strict with regard to such imperatives as "love that which pertains to your neighbor as if it pertains to yourself," actually indulges in the same process as the Reform! This may be a hard pill for the Orthodox to swallow.

The Orthodox would fiercely reject the Reform proposal that all individuals be presented the full range of Jewish observance and then be allowed to decide for themselves which parts they desire to observe and which parts they do not. Judaism is not optional; it is unconditional commitment. But if it is unconditional commitment, it is commitment to all the norms, including the norms that prescribe interpersonal relations. To be lax in that regard, albeit sometimes as a subconscious choice, it to indulge in the same practice as Reform, that of making value judgments concerning what is important in the Torah and what is not. It is choosing *from* the tradition rather than choosing *the* tradition.

The mere emphasis on the ethical sphere in Reform does not guarantee that every individual in the Reform community is better honed in the ethical sphere. The emphasis only speaks of a philosophy and a sense of where one's energy need be directed. There is no question that the ethical is a sphere which needs to be perfected, be it within Reform, be it within Conservative, be it within Orthodox Judaism. However, it remains the case that where one sees an Orthodox Jew who is delinquent in interpersonal relations, it hurts more because one expects better from an individual who purports to represent all that is contained in the Torah.

Ideally, the philosophical construct that seems to be projected by the Torah is one in which the ritual side of observance and the ethical side are mutually reinforcing. For example, the notion of kindness to the species and the prevention of unnecessary cruelty to animals is the human fulfillment side, the counterpart of which is embodied in a daily practice which actually lives that philosophy. That practice is none other than the requirements which must be met for any meat to be considered kosher.

Kosher meat is essentially meat that has been prepared with the most scrupulous attention to avoiding unnecessary pain to the animal in the process of it being ritually slaughtered. It is not an accident that in Jewish life those individuals who prepare the meat from slaughtering and on are knowledgeable, peace-loving individuals who do not go about shooting or hunting for thrills. They are very meticulous in the way they prepare the meat or fowl which will be consumed by the Jewish community.

We may speak, philosophically, about the dignity of the human being, and the need to avoid reducing the human being to mere property, or to a means toward an end. The Shabbat, which divorces the regular week-day activity from the seventh day, and insists that on the seventh day the human being indulge in no material creativity, and instead concentrate on and celebrate the human side of life, is a ritualistic fulfillment of this very noble ideal.

One could go through the entire corpus of Jewish law and find the mutually reinforcing connections between the ritual side and the human side, between the person-God dimensions and the person-to-person dimensions. When commandments are lived within this mutually reinforcing dimension, they become alive and vibrant with the very spirit of life.

However, when these dimensions are not mutually reinforcing, they become compartmentalized off from one another. The ritual side is neglected, and the ethical side is suffocated for lack of transcending inspiration. Or, the ethical side gets neglected, and the ritual side takes on a different coloration. Instead of it being an affirmation of life, ritual then degenerates into an exercise in denial. It reduces itself to a perfunctory exercise of obligation, with little spontaneity or vitality. It is unfortunate that too many people have in their minds the vision of a religious person as being austere, stern, severe, leaning towards self-denial and privation rather than towards affirmation of life in joy, even in ecstasy.

There is something to be said for an educational system that emphasizes to its students the notion of "having to" observe, but imposing the notion of "having to" on its own does not inspire the way Torah was intended to inspire. There is a "having to" aspect to Jewish observance, but this "having to" needs to be complemented with the notion of "wanting to," of desiring to observe because it is inspiring, because it is uplifting, because it is ennobling. "Having to," in spite of *not* "wanting to," conjures up the notion of denial of the self in order to satisfy God.

However, denial as a normative expression is at once a distortion of the Godly ideal and the human imperative. It conceives of a God who needs to be appeased, even spoon fed, and postulates a human reality in which all wrongdoing can be wiped away by an act of denial instead of the human act of repentance. Authentic Judaism asks for purity of heart and sincerity of purpose, consistent with divine dictates, to be the operating dynamic of behavior. This invests life with the proper meaning. Failing that, any action is a mechanistic response easily replicated by a robot.

The upshot of a lifestyle which views religious expression as denial is that one develops a negative view of God as a punishing, demanding being, and a view of life as full of ugly enticements which must be avoided if one is to be considered meritorious. Not only is this personally debilitating, in that it encourages a melancholy attitude to life; it is a repulsive model wih serves only to discourage the masses from adhering to traditional norms.

There is an old story of two friends who, having sinned together, decided they would visit their local Rabbi in tandem to confess their sin and ask for an appropriate strategy for penitence. After hearing the case, the Rabbi recommended that they should go about their regular business for the next week with peas in their shoes. In mid week, the partners in sin met. One was moving about in considerable pain, the other went around as if nothing had changed. The in-pain partner angrily accused his counterpart of openly rebelling against the Rabbinic charge. The partner protested, insisting that he was following the Rabbi's directions to the letter. "Then why are you not in pain if you have peas in your shoes?" he asked. The response came fast and sure; "I cooked them first!"

There is no magic in walking around with cooked peas, but there is also no magic in going around with hard peas, unless the pain experienced with every step is a behavior conditioner, reminding the person at every turn to avoid wrong and accent the right. It is only when denial relates to affirming life, when it leads to a more wholesome embrace of life's contingencies, that it can be countenanced as a necessary component of the human endeavor. In other words, a guilt "trip" is not so bad if it will ultimately lead the person to a worthwhile destination.

Judaism is in fact a celebration of life in its multi-dimensional sense. It is a lifestyle of joy rather than a depressing set of rituals. It is designed to make the practitioner of Jewish norms alert to the world, alive to responsibility, and sensitive to others. Where this fails to evolve, there is something dismally wrong with whatever observance is being practiced. On the other hand, Jewish ethics cannot exist on their own, but need to be constantly reinforced by ritual practices, which impress the individual with the source of the ethical imperative, and thus make ethical expression a transcending act.

Orthodoxy needs to look seriously at itself, and to ask whether it represents the Torah as completely as it claims. It needs to look closely at the hard fact that more than three-quarters of the North American Jewish community distances itself and is alienated from Orthodox practice. Reform does not exist in a vacuum; it has found a receptive home amongst too many who feel that the Judaism of the right is not the right Judaism.

114

There is no instance in Jewish law where pain is mandated for pain sake. There are situations when an individual is asked to desist from certain pleasures, such as on the Day of Atonement, but the thrust of the denial is not to simply remove oneself from the pleasure aspect of reality. On the Day of Atonement, the denial is intended to take the individual away from material concerns of any sort, and to thrust the individual into a confrontation with the self which will result in an improved person. The marital cycle, with its period of abstinence, is not mandated in order that the couple be removed from sensual pleasure. The marital prescription attempts to ensure that the wife not be reduced to a sexual object, and that there is a heightened sense of renewal which reinvigorates the marital union from month to month. This renewal is effected through the potentially exhilarating experience of immersing oneself in the ritual bath called mikvah. The mikvah envelopes the body, freshens in a spiritual as well as a physical sense, and readies one for renewed commitment.

The mikvah has been wrongly identified as a bastion of denial, when in effect it is a monument and a testimony to reinvigoration and revitalization. The obligation to immerse in the mikvah following the seven-day aftermath of menstruation is a prelude to sexual fulfillment, not the climax of a period of denial. The husband's obligation to be alert to his wife's expectations at this moment is one of the most vital legal components of marriage. The mikvah symbolizes renewal, and releases the sensual energy that enhances the love relationship.

It is in this very mikvah where conversion is finalized, both for the male and the female. For the non-Jew who is becoming Jewish, the mikvah can and should be the symbol of a new life and a new reality; an emergence from the womb of Jewish theology, the ritual bath, into a new world. Perceived as such, mikvah is not an archaic institution at all, but an institution that sanctifies and hallows every organ of the body, every moment of life.

If Orthodoxy were to project its religious practices with a sense of joy, such institutions as mikvah could be more easily adopted as normative for conversion by the Reform. By addressing the critical questions that presently confront the North American Jewish community, one of them being conversion, in a spirit of togetherness, a more profound appreciation of the thrust of tradition, stemming from an enlightened awareness, will open up new avenues of expression for the Reform, and new understanding and fresh appreciation of tradition in its most vibrant sense. But Reform can only reach that point with the help of the Orthodox, with their understanding and abiding friendship.

With regard to divorce, it may be surprising, but in Jewish tradition the writing of a bill of divorce delivered by the husband to his wife upon termination of the marriage is the fulfillment of a mitzvah, much like the wearing of a garment with fringes (talit) is a fulfillment of a mitzvah. This does not mean that it is a mitzvah to divorce your spouse. It means that if divorce becomes an inescapable reality, it is a mitzvah to effect this reality through a bill of divorce called get.

What is the magical about a get? Surely it is not a joyful occasion when a couple divorces, but the get need not be a melancholy experience. It can be a meaningful occasion. And the meaningfulness in a divorce inheres in that it is written and delivered in an aura of sanctity. The document that is transmitted from husband to wife is a sacred document written by a scribe in the same lettering as a Torah itself is written. This cannot but impress the couple that the sanctity of life, reflected in the Jewish affirmation of life's contingencies, relates even to unfortunate circumstances.

The granting of divorce need not be an expression of inequality between male and female, nor need it be an embarrassing experience for the woman. Properly arranged and effected, the get at once laments the failures of the past and opens up avenues for future fulfillment. There is no question in my mind that the Rabbis who supervise the granting of divorce need to convey to the parting couple the sanctity of life, and the possibilities for future joy which emerge upon termination of the failed marital experience. If this is conveyed effectively, the get procedure can become an uplifting experience for all parties concerned.

And with the proliferation of divorce today, the Jewish community simply cannot afford a situation where every divorce becomes a war. So, in the sacred atmosphere of a Rabbinic setting, it is equally incumbent upon the Rabbis to try to make the divorce a peaceful parting of the ways in which coexistence, albeit from a distance, is possible in the future, especially when there are children involved.

Here too, how a basic norm is projected can impact heavily on its acceptability by the Reform. The Orthodox need not think of this as a compromise, but rather as the right way of doing things in the first place. But handling get procedures with a meaningful thrust will undoubtedly make it much more palatable for Reform to embrace the theological clearing house notion of divorce previously proposed. Such embrace will serve to avoid so many questions of legitimacy that ultimately threaten to divide and destroy the North American Jewish community.

The interchange between the Orthodox and the Reform can greatly enhance the future of the North American Jewish community, if both groups go about the business of interchange committed to the community rather than to parochial interests. It is obvious from the excitement that is experienced within Orthodox ranks when an individual returns from near assimilation that the Orthodox are very much concerned about the future of the North American Jewish community. However, the returns to Orthodoxy from assimilation, or from something less than Orthodoxy, are really a drop in the bucket measured against the possibly three million or more Jews in danger of assimilation.

Orthodoxy cannot wait for things to happen. Instead, Orthodoxy needs to aggressively pursue its concern for the future of the Jewish community. The only way that it can resourcefully do this is by taking it from the top, by reinvestigating its past policies with regard to communication with Reform leadership, and reaching the conclusion that in the interest of the community's future, and consistent with Judaism's concern for the entire Jewish community, Orthodoxy must work together with the Reform to come up with uncompromising but workable solutions to avoid the coming cataclysm. And, if Orthodoxy and Reform can come together, the Conservatives will assuredly and gladly join the new alignment.

In Biblical literature there are many census takings which are reported. The Bible, as is well known, is not a sociological document. Then why a census? There is theological significance to the census taking, in that the numbers that are counted project the most timely message that each and every individual counts. If there is one individual who has not been counted, or who cannot be counted, then the community is deficient. A community of six hundred and three thousand, five hundred and fifty, is a total community; a community of six hundred and three thousand, five hundred and forty nine is a deficient community. This may be the theological and human significance of a census.

If we approach the Jewish reality of North America in the Biblical spirit, we will not be satisfied with lower rates of divorce or lower rates of assimilation. In the same way as we aspire for the ultimate in personal observance, we need to aspire for the ultimate in communal solidarity and spirituality. The most meaningful statistic in a Jewish census is that everyone is counted in the fold. Today the obligation and the imperative to make this possible is a herculian task which demands massive reorientation and united, energetic effort. Is Orthodoxy capable of playing its proper role in this endeavor? The answer to this question will impact heavily not only on the future of Orthodoxy, but also on the future of Judaism in North America.

117

CHAPTER 15
THE JEWISH FUTURE

Tradition has it that just prior to the transmission of the Torah on Mount Sinai, the Israelite community was united as one in excitement, looking forward to the great event. However, immediately following receipt of the Torah, that unity splintered, primarily because there were divergent interpretations of what the Torah meant and how it was to be applied. There was thus unity in anticipation, but division in interpretation.

This being the case, it should hardly be surprising and is even understandable that so many years removed from Sinai there should be diametrically opposite interpretations of the Torah, even the rejection of the Torah itself. Up until the present moment, Judaism has literally been a history of cleavage and attempted rapprochement, of confusion followed by fusion followed by confusion again. There have been only precious few moments in Jewish history when the entire Jewish population was united under one common ideology and actually practiced one common code of behavior.

The pushes and pulls on the Jewish community from within and without have elicited interesting responses from the Jewish community. Thanks to the threat of the Karaites, we have some incisive contributions from Saadia Gaon, including the "Book of Beliefs and Opinions." Thanks to the threat posed by the culture in which he lived, we have some great works by Maimonides, among them the "Guide for the Perplexed." Thanks in no small measure to the threat of Reform, we have some significant treatises by Samson Raphael Hirsch, such as "Horeb." Today, as a result of the threat of assimilation, amongst other dangers confronting the Jewish community, we have an endless supply of books about the Jewish heritage, Jewish belief, and Jewish practice. The tension within the community has thus not been without advantage.

Obviously many would prefer that Judaism travel forth from generation to generation without such challenges either from within or from without. But Judaism, on balance, has actually strengthened itself through the way in which it has confronted the challenges of the past.

However, it is the thesis of this presentation that Judaism today faces a challenge which is unique in its history, both in degree and in kind. The birth of Christianity did not cause great defections from Jewish ranks. The Karaite rebellion did not make an appreciable dent in the Jewish community. The Sabbatean movement with its messianic overtones, impacted on a significant number, yet did not really threaten the fabric of the Jewish community down the road.

But in twentieth century North America, Judaism is threatened from within, not from without. There is no oppressive government or marauding crusader who can be blamed for the ills that plague Judaism. This time we have done it to ourselves, or at least we are on the way to doing it. It is not too late to act, but it is too late to delay from confronting the issues. Procrastination at this point in time only makes the doom and gloom predictions for tomorrow all the more realistic.

Some of these doom and gloom predictions include the following: 1) One out of every two Jews who marry in the 1980's will be divorced by 1990; 2) one out of every two Jewish college students who marry in the 1980's will marry out of the faith; 3) one out of every two Jewish families will have no synagogue or Jewish organization affiliation; 4) 40% of Jewish children will receive no Jewish education, and will not even have a Bar or Bat Mitzvah.

This is a fire-alarm crisis which demands a fire-alarm response, without delay, without pettiness, without compromise.

There is one critical ingredient which we will need in large quantity over the course of the next few decades. We will need the consummate courage of the leadership within Orthodoxy, Conservative and Reform Judaism. Megadoses of courage will be demanded if we are to transcend the entrenched positions of the past, if we are to rise above the antipathies that have surfaced in abundance in the last decades, if we are to confront the future with dedication to effecting one reality over and above any other – the survival and flourishing of the total Jewish community, within the context of Jewish tradition.

Of immediacy in this endeavor of common courage is the need to confront the conversion and divorce dilemmas, what with their resultant impact in terms of the Jewishness of the Jewish community, and the legitimacy of its Jews. The working proposal suggested herein, of a theological clearing house under the common administration of the Orthodox, Conservative and Reform Rabbinates, with a Rabbinical court to serve the clearing house and working within the parameters of halakhah, stripped of unnecessary stringency but clearly committed to the esence and thrust of the halakhah, would go a long way towards resolving the crisis.

But there is more than just resolving the crisis that could be achieved with this new framework. At this most critical time in the history of the Jewish people, we will have created a framework which can potentially usher in a new era of cooperation, coexistence, cross fertilization of ideas, and mutually reinforced concern for all. If the Orthodox, Conservative, and Reform can agree on a common policy for divorce and conversion, then perhaps we can take this common agreement one step further.

To take it one step further in this instance means to go all the way back to the pre-Sinai experience, when in anticipation of receiving the Torah, the entire community was unified. What we

119

need at the present moment is to anticipate a renewal, a new beginning of sorts, a looking back at where we have been, what our policies have wrought, where Judaism is headed; and then to make a midcourse correction in the form of a revelation to the entire North American Jewish community, telling them where they are, and what they can be. But, like the revelation from Sinai, it needs to come from the top.

We do not need a new Torah, but we do need a renewal of commitment to the Torah and its values. In this regard, Reform has actually opened up its doors to Torah in an unprecedented change reflected in the Centenary Perspective. By asking that all of its members make an enlightened choice of what aspects of Judaism they would want to actualize, after having carefully studied all the options, Reform is willy-nilly opening up the Orthodox option to its constituents.

It is this framework which perhaps can work for the entire North American Jewish community. Let the community be presented with the broad smorgasbord of Jewish tradition in its unadulterated, pristine beauty. Let that be the Judaism of the ideal standards, let that be the summum bonum. Let there in fact be just one Judaism, the ideal Judaism that was given from Mount Sinai and which would be presented as the full course menu for the North American Jewish community.

Undoubtedly, we will have those who take the full course, those who skip the entree and the dessert, those who also may even skip the main course. But at least they will all be invited to the banquet. And, they will all have an equal share in exposure to Judaism. There will always be different types of Jews. It should be enough for a person to say "I am a Jew," and not have to answer to the question what type of Jew – Orthodox, Conservative, Reform, hermaphrodite, etc. Different brands of Judaism have brought us to the brink of catastrophe, and the best way to redress this situation is to cut it off at the roots.

Reform has made its impact, it has delivered a message, and Orthodoxy has hopefully heard loud and clear the essence of the message. Now, by working together, a consensual Judaism can appear on the scene which will be an inspiration to the masses, and may even be exciting enough to ward off the threat of mass defections.

Orthodox, Conservative, and Reform working together – it is a dream, but the flip side of the dream is a nightmare. If the leadership in these sectors cannot transcend the encumbrances of the past, the Jewish community itself should rise up and *demand* that the leaders work together. If all avenues fail, we may soon not have a true Jewish community to speak of.

Working together, the Orthodox, Conservative, and Reform can launch a massive assault on the main problem facing them squarely in the eye, the ignorance and indifference of a great percentage of North America's Jews. If these Jews see that the leaders care, and care together, they may be inspired to be part of a vibrant, united community, when before they may have been disenchanted by the petty chauvinisms of the disparate branches comprising the Jewish community.

A positive fallout of the Orthodox-Conservative-Reform alliance to save the North American Jewish community is that the internecine strife in Israel between these sectors, which threatens to engulf Israel in a totally divisive, unnecessary rift, may be forestalled. Beleaguered Israel can ill afford internal cleavage amongst the religious groups. If the three sectors can form a common front regarding conversion and divorce in North America, it may be possible to achieve a similar modus operandi in Israel.

There is a story in the Talmud about a Rabbi who insisted that only students whose inner personalities were consistent with their outer behavior should be allowed to enter into the academic institution to study. This Rabbi wanted to prevent individuals of less than pure character from entering the academic study hall, the Yeshiva, lest these people contaminate the rest of the student population.

However, when this head of the academy was removed, and a new Dean took over the institution, he abolished this restrictive policy, and allowed anyone who wished to study to enter the academy. That day, according to the Talmud, many more benches, many more students, were added to the academy. According to one view, four hundred benches were added; according to another, seven hundred benches were added. Clearly, an argument about whether there were four hundred or seven hundred benches added seems to be a little bit odd. To settle the argument, all one had to do was to get a decent count. And, the difference between four hundred and seven hundred is significant enough that it is hard to comprehend how this could have even been a matter of dispute.

Possibly then, there was no question that prior to the open door policy, the academy was comprised of three hundred benches. When the academy opened its doors wide, the population expanded almost immediately to seven hundred benches. The difference of opinion in the Talmud is not on the fact of the matter, but rather on the impact of the matter. According to one view, four hundred benches were added, and that is all.

However, according to the other view, the four hundred benches were added to the previous three hundred benches, making now for a total of seven hundred, but for a totally new seven hundred, a totally different academic institution. Because, contrary to the fears underlying the restrictive policy of the original academic head, the opening up of the doors to anyone who wanted to be part of the academy even though possibly not up to academic standards, created a situation which impacted positively on the previously well entrenched and staid students. Now being confronted with challenging dialogue by a group that came in fresh, maybe even from the street, they began to see new perspectives, they began to see new approaches. Their entire understanding of reality and how Judaism relates to that reality became revitalized. So, in the second view, there may have been four hundred new additions, but it made for an entirely new academy, a better academy at that.

That episode and its message can be applied to the situation today in the North American Jewish community. The addition to the communal matrix of an entire sector or entire sectors of the Jewish community will impact heavily and positively on those sectors which are presently entrenched in their respective communal positions. Reform exposure to Orthodoxy cannot help but give Reform an even greater appreciation of Jewish tradition. Orthodox exposure to Reform cannot help but open Orthodoxy up to the types of concerns pre-occupying Reform, the difficulties that Reform has experienced in the past with religious categories, and how these differences can perhaps be mediated through meaningful dialogue and insightful education. Reform emphasis on decorum should also be a welcome addition to the Orthodox community.

Individuals who profess to belief in God on a profound level have no difficulty with the existence of some problematic realities, such as evil or boredom. Boredom, they would say, is specifically in place as a feeling of emptiness which, when felt, goads the individual to overcome the boredom through meaningful action. Evil, whilst not welcome, is the dark side of human potential, and allows for the element of choice; choice being that which makes every action of the human being not a programmed robot-like response, but a free-willed act of a deciding being. The possibility for evil makes the choice for good a true human endeavor. With no choice there is no meaningful existence.

But how does a religious person reconcile the existence of atheism? Is not atheism the very antithesis of the God idea? How, then, could such an idea exist? Some insightful Rabbis have in the past made some interesting observations concerning atheism. They have said that there are times in one's life when one *must* be an atheist.

For example, if a poor man should knock on your door and ask for help because he has nothing to eat, you should not, at that point in time, profess faith in God by saying to the poor man – I know that you are hungry and that you have nothing to eat, but trust in God who sustains all poor people; as a matter of fact God sustains all human kind. God is sure to help you at some point or another.

That is an exercise of faith which is a distortion of the God idea. At that point in time an individual should become an atheist, and should say that God is not going to help the poor person; instead the responsibility rests on my shoulders to intervene, to help that individual and rescue him from his hunger.

Similarily, on a communal level, there are times when individuals or groups must intervene, and not wait for or rely on divine visitation. In this sense we should all see ourselves as atheists, and suspend the idea that God will help us out of the mess that we created. We must not rely on God to initiate the proper response to the dilemmas that are confronting us. We, in our holy atheism, must begin the process ourselves, in the hope that having started to tackle the issues, we will be aided and spirited by the realization that success in this matter will mean the salvation of the Jewish people. Paradoxically, the atheist-like resolve in this issue is the most noble affirmation of God and the Jewish idea.

BIBLIOGRAPHY

Angel, M. Another Halakhic Approach to Conversions. *Tradition*, 12 (3-4), Winter-Spring 1972, 107-113.

Angel, M. Orthodoxy in Isolation. *Moment*, 5 (8), September 1980, 61-62.

Bergman, E. The American Jewish Population Erosion. *Midstream*, 23 (8), October 1977, 9-19.

Berkovits, E. *Crisis and Faith*. New York; Sanhedrin Press, 1976.

Berkovits, E. *Not in Heaven; The Nature and Function of Halakha*. New York: Ktav Publishing House, 1983.

Blau, J. *Modern Varieties of Judaism*. New York: Columbia University Press, 1964.

Bleich, J. *Contemporary Halakhic Problems*. New York: Ktav Publishing House, 1977.

Bleich, J. Parameters and Limits of Communal Unity from the Perspective of Jewish Law. *Journal of Halacha and Contemporary Society*, 6, Fall 1983, 5-20.

Borowitz, E. *Reform Judaism Today* (3 vols.). New York: Behrman House, 1978.

Bulka, R. (Ed.). *Dimensions of Orthodox Judaism*. New York: Ktav Publishing House, 1983.

Conversion and Patrilineality. Special section of *Intermountain Jewish News*, December 2, 1983.

Elazar, D. *Community and Polity: The Organizational Dynamics of American Jewry*. Philadelphia: Jewish Publication Society, 1976.

Hofstein, S. Perspectives on the Jewish Single-Parent Family. *Journal of Jewish Communal Service*, 1978, 54 (3), 229-240.

Jakobovits, I. *The Timely and the Timeless: Jews, Judaism and Society in a Storm-tossed Decade*. London: Vallentine, Mitchell, 1977.

Lieberman, S. & Weinfeld, M. Demographic Trends and Jewish Survival. *Midstream*, 24 (9), November 1978, 9-19.

Liebman, C. *The Ambivalent American Jew: Politics, Religion, and Family in American Jewish Life*. Philadelphia: Jewish Publication Society, 1976.

Mandelbaum, B. The Right to be Different. *Tradition*, 12 (3-4), Winter-Spring 1972, 35-42.

Maslin, S. (Ed.). *Gates of Mitzvah: A Guide to the Jewish Life Cycle*. New York: Central Conference of American Rabbis, 1979.

Massarik, F. *Intermarriage: Facts for Planning*. New York: Council of Jewish Federations and Welfare Funds, no date.

Neusner, J. (Ed.). *Understanding American Judaism: Toward the Description of a Modern Religion* (2 vols.). New York: Ktav Publishing House, 1975.

Petuchowski, J. Plural Models within the Halakhah. *Judaism*, 19 (1), Winter 1979, 77-79.

Rudavsky, D. *Modern Jewish Religious Movements: A History of Emancipation and Adjustment*. New York: Behrman House, 1967.

Schlesinger, B. Jewish One-Parent Families: A Growing Phenomenon in the 1970's. *Journal of Psychology and Judaism*, Spring-Summer 1983, 7 (2), 89-100.

Spero, S. Orthodoxy vis-a-vis the General Community: Does Participation Imply Recognition? *Tradition*, 9 (4), Winter 1966, 55-64

Spero, S. A Rejoinder. *Tradition*, 12 (3-4), Winter-Spring 1972, 43-48.

Weiss, R. *Marital Separation*. New York: Basic Books, 1975.

Wurzburger, W. Plural Models and the Authority of the Halakhah. *Judaism*, 20 (4), Fall 1971, 390-395.

Index

Abortion, p. 37
Abraham, p. 26
Adulterous Jewish Union, p. 53
Adultery, p. 52, 53
Afghanistan, p. 106
Ahavat Yisrael, p. 62
Aliyah, p. 102
America, p. 31
American, p. 38
Amida, p. 88
Anti-Semitism, p. 21
Assimilation, p. 75, 117
Atheism, p. 122, 123
"B' Dee' Avad," p. 69
Baal Shem Tov, Israel, p. 83
Baal Tshuva, p. 33, 34
Bar Kokhba, p. 87
Bar Mitzvah, p. 50
Bastard, p. 54
Bat Mitzvah, p. 50
Begin, Menachem, p. 32
Besht, p. 83
Beth Din, p. 65
Bible, p. 19
Biblical, p. 26
Blood-Letting, p. 46
Book of Beliefs and Opinions, p. 118
Book of Geneological Pedigree, p. 71
Canada, p. 70
Candle Lighting, p. 27
Candles, p. 106
CCar, p. 50
Centenary Perspective, p. 102
Central Conference of American Rabbis, p. 50
Christianity, p. 85, 86
Christmas, p. 38
Church and State, p. 31
Church, p. 31, 92
Circumcision, p. 45
Civil Divorce, p. 53
Civil Rights, p. 28
Civil War, p. 59
Clearing House, p. 65

Code of Jewish Law, p. 26
Cohabitates, p. 53
Colombus Platform, p. 25, 102
Commandments, p. 46
Conservatism, p. 29, 61
Conservative Judaism, p. 13
Constantine, p. 88
Conversion, p. 44
Converts, p. 45
Convenant, p. 45
Convenantal, p. 45
Day of Atonement, p. 45
Denial, p. 113
Dietary Laws, p. 20
Divorce, p. 52, 53
Easter, p. 38
Ecstacy, p. 113
Ethical Humanism, p. 37
Fearers of the Lord, p. 86
Fertility, p. 38
Frankists, p. 43
Ganzfried, Shlomo, p. 60
Gaon, Saadia, p. 84, 118
Gaza, p. 26
Get, p. 52
Ghetto, p. 21
God, p. 26
Greek, p. 86
Guide for the Perplexed, p. 118
Halakhah, p. 45
Halakhic, p. 39
Hasidic, p. 35
Hasidism, p. 35, 83
Hatafat Dam Brit, p. 46
Havdalah, p. 60
Hebrew Christian, p. 92
Hirsch, Samson Raphael, p. 118
Holocaust, p. 95
Homosexuality, p. 37
Horeb, p. 118
Hupah, p. 55
Illegitimacy, p. 53, 70
Incestuous Jewish Union, p. 53
Intermarriage, p. 48, 49
Ironsides, p. 28

Israel, p. 23
Israelite, p. 49
Jerusalem, p. 20
Jesus, p. 87
Jewish Marriage, p. 55
Jewish Tradition, p. 46
Jewish, p. 38, 45, 123
Jews, p. 30, 44
Joy, p. 113
Judaic Tradition, p. 40
Judaic, p. 40
Judaism, p. 40, 96, 122
Judea, p. 26
Kabalat Hamitzvot, p. 45, 46, 76
Karaites, p. 43, 83
Karo, Yosef, p. 60
Kasruth, p. 23
Ketubah, p. 55
Kiddush, p. 27, 60
Kipa, p. 20
Kohen, p. 49
Kol D'Medadesh Ada'Ata D'Rabbanan Mekadesh, p. 55
Kosher, p. 22
Lebanon, p. 32
Legitimate, p. 47
Lekhatchila, p. 69
Levite, p. 49
Liberal, p. 31
Lubavitch, p. 108
Maccabean, p. 93
Maimonides, p. 118
Mamzer, p. 54
Mamzerim, p. 70
Mamzerut, p. 58
Marital Relations, p. 55
Marriage, Jewish, p. 55
Marriage, p. 38, 44, 49
Matrilineal, p. 49
Menstruant, p. 46
Messiah, p. 86-87
Mezuzah, p. 79
Mezuzot, p. 71
Mikvah, p. 45
Mitnagdim, p. 83
Mitzvah, p. 80

Mixed Marriage, p. 44
Mosaic, p. 61
Mt. Sinai, p. 19
National Geographic, p. 28
Nazis, p. 89
Neusner, J., p. 15
Neuturei Karta, p. 27, 108
New York City, p. 30
Non-Jewish, p. 44
North America, p. 71
North American Jewish Community, p. 13
North American Jewry, p. 59
Nuclear Disarmament, p. 31
Organ, p. 20
Orthodox Jews, p. 48
Orthodox Judaism, p. 21, 60
Orthodox Rabbi, p. 36, 48
Orthodoxy, p. 13
Orthoprax, p. 27
Out of Wedlock, p. 53
Palestine, p. 102
Passover, p. 38
Paul, p. 86
Peripherals, p. 34
Pharisees, p. 43
Pittsburgh Platform, p. 25
Privation, p. 113
Rabbi, p. 36
Rabbinical Council of America, p. 66
Rabbinical Court, p. 65, 73
Rabbinical Tribunal, p. 53
Rabbinism, p. 89
Reform Jews, p. 48
Reform Judaism, p. 14
Reform Rabbinate, p. 44
Reform Rabbis Council of Toronto, p. 50
Reform Rabbis, p. 36, 44
Reform, p. 13
Ritual Immersion, p. 46
Ritual Slaughterers, p. 71
Ritual, p. 45
Rome, p. 85
Russia, p. 31, 59
Russian Jewry, p. 96
Sabbateans, p. 43

Sadducees, p. 43
Samaria, p. 26
Schechter, Solomon, p. 22
Scribe, p. 53
Sefer Yuchsin, p. 71
Seminarians, p. 26
Shabbat, p. 27
Shaliach, p. 35
Shochtim, p. 71
Shtetl, p. 21
Shulhan Arukh, p. 60
Six Million, p. 97
Sofer, p. 53
Soviet Union, p. 30
State of Israel, p. 26
State, p. 31
Synagogue Council of America, p. 66
Talit, p. 20
Talmud, p. 19
Talmudic Judaism, p. 93
Talmudic, p. 52
Tefilin, p. 20
Temple, p. 20
Theological Clearing House, p. 66
Three Million, p. 97
Time, p. 34
Torah Scroll, p. 28, 60
Union of Orthodox Jewish Congregations, p. 66
United Jewish Appeal, p. 32
United States, p. 70
United Synagogue, p. 22
West Bank, p. 26
Who is a Jew, p. 43
Winn, Conrad, p. 9, 14
Yeshiva, p. 108
Yom Kippur, p. 38
Zero Population Growth, p. 38
Zion, p. 20
Zionism, p. 32, 108